The Heroine's Journey

The Heroine's Journey

My Story and Your Guide to Unleashing the Heroine Within

Kerri Cust

ISBN-13: 9781539968740
ISBN-10: 153996874X

For Nicholas

Welcome

HELLO YOU BRAVE and beautiful soul!

You must be looking for more from life. Something is calling you, isn't it?

You are feeling the pull.

This book has shown up in your hands to assist you with stepping out towards a new, more fulfilling life. Throughout these pages, I share my own venture out to the unknown and the lessons I learned along the way so you can take advantage of my wisdom and tools without having to follow the long and bumpy path that was my experience.

It is my recommendation that you read the chapters and complete the exercises in the order they are presented because each one creates a critical foundation as you move on to the following lesson. The worksheets and activities following each chapter are quite powerful; it is important to devote time and attention to each of them to ensure you get the most out of each exercise. Make sure you do your homework!

My suggestion is to not do more than one chapter per day. This way you have the time to really allow the lessons to integrate in to your consciousness and being. I would even recommend meditating after you have completed each exercise; this will assist the absorption of the information and awareness you have gained.

May this book be used to its highest potential; may it serve your life and move you towards the life that God is waiting for you to live out.

May God's will be done.

Table of Contents

CHAPTER 1

— ✀ —

A Brief History

I WASN'T ALWAYS the tantric, spiritualist, hippie divorcee that I am today, writing all of my stories down and documenting every wild experience of my world. How I got to that point is a story unto itself.

I thought that I was living the dream, doing what everyone was supposed to do. I went to college, I got married; I became a business professional and home owner with children just around the corner. It was ultimate conventional life, and everything was happening exactly as expected. Then I realized that convention just wasn't going to work for me and everything changed. Suddenly, I was single, unemployed and living on the other side of the world with no clue what my life was going to look like months or weeks down the line.

The journey that began as I approached my 30th birthday has required me to shed and change almost everything about myself. As you read on, I hope you are inspired to blossom into exactly who you were meant to be. I share the pieces of my life that lead up to the evening when everything changed — when I left my marriage and began to transform into the Heroine I was always destined to become.

My own birth was the result of a summer romance and therefore completely unplanned. My mother was in her very early twenties and my biological father was just nineteen; they were both living in the same small town in Canada. I was born on June 11, 1985, and my father chose not to be in my life, so I was raised by my mother with the help of my grandparents. We moved around a lot, but I mainly grew up in a small town in Alberta, Canada.

As you can imagine, I grew up with those "Daddy Issues" that everyone talks about. I craved for my father to be a part of and even save me from my life, which in my late teens and early twenties manifested as attracting unavailable men.

One thing that I inherited from both my mother and father is the desire for adventure. Both are teachers and have chosen to travel and teach overseas. Although there wasn't much travel in my upbringing, this genetic disposition would definitely manifest later on in my life.

When I was three years old, my mother met a man who she eventually married, and together, they had my two brothers. I didn't like my stepfather when I initially met him, but after chocolate and ice cream (always a way to my heart), I warmed up to him and began calling him dad.

The relationship between my mother and stepfather was turbulent (to say the least), and they were on and off many times throughout the course of their relationship. By no means was theirs a healthy relationship to model, but despite the difficulties, I grew to love him.

There were a lot of things I heard, witnessed and experienced that no child should ever have to go through. Now, I'm not naïve, and I know many people had it way harder than I did growing up, but the things I witnessed and the adult responsibilities I was given definitely contributed to my maturing very quickly.

There is a large age gap between me and my brothers. John is six years younger than I am, and Nicholas eleven years younger. Growing up with a (mostly) single mother (whenever my stepdad was out of the picture), I became the other parent, burdened by the responsibilities of looking after my brothers, keeping up the house, and everything else that grown-ups are supposed to do.

Nicholas and I in particular had a special bond. I was there when he was born, and the type of love I felt for him was unlike anything I had experienced before. I often thought to myself "This is what it must feel like to have a child."

When I was a pre-teen, I walked around with my baby brother on my hip, getting interesting stares from strangers. The love I had for Nicholas wasn't a love that is typical between siblings; in many ways I was his mother and he was my son. Although this role was a big one, I wouldn't have had it any other way.

John and I had a different type of relationship. He was very close to his dad (my stepfather), and it was my experience that John was preferred over me, which ignited my insecurities of being unworthy and feeling unwanted. The relationship between the two of us was fiery, to say the least, but cooled and settled as we got older. We are extremely different people, but I love him unconditionally.

There are a few incidents that occurred outside of my family life that had a big impact on me. When I was in the second grade, my mother, John and I were a car accident, hit by a half-ton truck. The truck hit my side of the car and left me with a concussion and a night in the hospital.

Within that same school year I experienced a severe dog attack at my after-school babysitter, and I was rushed to the hospital where a plastic surgeon placed close to 100 stitches in my face. I forgot to mention that I was born with a large birthmark that covers my entire left arm, which again plagued me (and still does) with insecurities. All of these things placed tiny marks of self-doubt and defeatism inside of me that I just couldn't overcome.

Although my childhood was definitely filled with drama, it also showed me my strengths and how much I could handle, which would come in handy in my late twenties.

As I moved into my late teens, like most teenagers I left home and attended my first year of college not knowing what the hell I wanted to do with my life. My first year of college, again like most first year students, was spent taking random courses amongst my excessive partying and drinking.

During this time, I was hungry for a relationship with a man, but all I was attracting were non-committal men who just wanted to have a good time. I willingly partook in this even though I was seeking something more from them.

Throughout my first year in college I made close, bonding relationships with a few female friends; these connections were something I had never experienced before. I viewed these women as my family, and I wanted them in my life for years to come. However, towards the end of the year, all of my girlfriends entered romantic relationships, and I quickly noticed how the dynamics changed. I felt as though our friendships were no longer on the same priority level. I was devastated by this and found it difficult to open up to female friendships for the next ten years.

After my first year of college, I still didn't know what I wanted to do with my life, and so I tried many things. I moved to another city, which didn't work out, so I ended up moving to yet another city and getting a job at the age of 21. Then I met my future husband.

One evening while I was out with a girlfriend, a very cute man, just a couple of years older than me, approached me in a bar and asked me for my phone number. I gave it to him, of course, and he called me the next day and we had our first date.

Very soon after we started dating, we became exclusive, and a few weeks later we exchanged 'I love you's.' It wasn't long before the 'we're going to get married' talk happened, and a few months after that we moved in together. Everything felt right and I really did love him.

He was a successful professional and there was a bit of pressure for me to get a 'stable' job, so I went back to school and got my business degree. I was heading towards the 'traditional' path, which at the time I was happy about. I craved stability, and if I was truly being honest with myself I didn't want to be like my mother. I wanted to 'have it all together' before the age of 30: the man, the job, the house, the kids, etc. I was well on my way, and on my 25th birthday, after nearly four years together, we got engaged.

There were small, subtle red flags throughout our relationship that often made me wonder, 'How was this going to work when we're married?' 'Am I willing to put up with this forever?' and 'What does this look like when we have children?', but because nothing was really wrong I continued on with the status quo.

Since I was so committed to creating a stable and 'picture perfect' life, I was determined that I was only going to be married once and it would be forever, so I made my fiancé go to pre-marriage counseling. Around this time, things started to feel a bit 'off,' and I started to experience some depression, which I blamed on my being in university while working part time. During a lunch break while we were in our pre-marriage counseling, my depression came up in conversation and I shared my thoughts that perhaps my studies weren't the only thing contributing to my depression; perhaps it was something else, including our relationship. My partner looked at me and asked what would happen if our working on it didn't help to heal the depression, and I looked at him and said, 'I don't know.' He cried. I immediately ran over to him, unable to bear the pain that I had caused someone I loved, and reassured him that I thought we could work on and get through it.

We were married just over a year after that. The wedding wasn't what I wanted, but it was a beautiful day. So began my traditional life. I finished school and began working at a good job. I had the husband, and next step was to buy a home and fill it with children.

From the outside, I had or at least was on my way to having it all. Life was routine, pretty uneventful, not great but not bad, and upon reflection it was very mediocre.

Just after my 28th birthday, we bought a house, and I think that's what made me finally be honest with myself and really look at whether this was the road I wanted to go down, to enter in my choice point.

CHAPTER 2

The Choice Point

I FINALLY ALLOWED myself to question and wonder if the reason I was unhappy and depressed was because I was in a relationship that I no longer wanted to be in. That single thought terrified me. The last thing I would ever want to do is hurt someone, especially someone I cared about.

One day I was visiting a spiritual bookstore with my mom and while looking through the books, I came across a set of angel cards and decided to ask some questions related to my marriage. I didn't get the answer I wanted (how could I have?), and I kept asking questions over and over again. Finally, with my mother sitting beside me, I began to cry, and she immediately asked what was wrong. I finally said the words out loud: "I don't think I want to be married anymore."

She was shocked, but then she said, "I've been there before."

It was an important moment but we couldn't talk more because we had to leave quickly to pick up my brother and then meet my husband at the house he and I had just purchased.

I found myself sitting in a big empty home that I was supposed to be moving into, with people walking around complimenting the house and congratulating both my husband and me on our new purchase.

I was sitting there questioning my life: how did I let myself get here? How could I allow it to get to this point? What was I going to do? Even though these questions were difficult, by asking them I felt as though I had finally awakened. But the painful part was that my husband had no idea.

The knowingness within me was unwavering. I gave myself time to reflect in that, secretly hoping that something would change and I wouldn't have to make the heart-wrenching decision that was in front of me. I spoke with many different therapists over a period of a week, explaining my situation, and they all said the same thing to me.

"It sounds like you've already made up your mind."

It was true; I knew I needed to leave my marriage.

My brother Nicholas and I were especially close, and he also had a good relationship with my husband. I was concerned how Nicholas might take the news. My mom shared with him what I was going through, and I received a beautiful message from him. Nicholas, 17 at the time, told me that I needed to trust my intuition and do what I needed to do. He mentioned that all he wanted was for his wonderful sister to be happy and told me that I would make the best decision. He went on to tell me that I was beautiful and gorgeous and that I'd never know how much I meant to him. This brought so much comfort to me during a time of fear, uncertainty and inner turmoil.

It was time. I knew without a flicker of doubt what I needed to do. Now it was time to actually do it, and so I did. Leaving my marriage was the hardest thing I've ever had to do. Even though I knew it was right, I cried through the pain I felt and the pain I was causing someone else.

Never in our nearly seven years together had I seen my husband in the state that he was in. Even amongst his pain and my own I knew it was the right decision.

The following week was hard, and I continually beat myself up with 'should's'; I should stay, we should go to therapy, I should work on the marriage, but I couldn't deny my truth.

I moved out of the apartment we shared and moved, temporarily, into the big house we had just purchased that was now back up for sale.

There I was again: alone in a big empty house that symbolized and mirrored back to me the loneliness I was feeling, perhaps the loneliness that had always been there but that had finally presented itself in a way I could no longer ignore.

The Choice Point Exercise
Theme: Trust

———— ୭୦ ————

SOMETHING WAS CALLING me, and I knew I had to follow it, scary as it was. I knew if I didn't answer the call a part of me would die. There were many good reasons why I shouldn't have left my marriage and why I should have stayed and moved into the big home we had just bought. However, a small but constant voice within was asking me to step up. Although I had always been a spiritual person, I was being called to new depths. I had to follow that pull, and I needed trust to do it.

The following exercises will help you to become aware of and cultivate trust in yourself and God.

1. Remember a time when you felt really guided by something outside yourself. What was the situation and how did you feel? How did you know you were taken care of and how did you know you were exactly where you needed to be?
2. Remember a time when something within you just knew what you had to do - to make a specific choice or go in a specific direction, regardless of the advice and suggestions of others. What conditions made it possible to hear your inner voice and trust yourself?
3. In what ways do you trust yourself:
   I trust myself to _____
4. In what ways do you trust God/the Universe?
   I trust God/the Universe to _____

Take Action!

Now that you remember and know that you can trust yourself and God, it's time to take action. Know that in order to step up and into a new life and way of being a choice and action must be taken.

So your homework is to follow your own intuition and inner knowing about something you have been facing, or anything, big or small that may arise in the next few days. Choose to follow your knowing.

Choose a situation in your life that is causing you worry or a dis-ease and ask and invite God in to provide help. As you ask for help and surrender the situation to God, be ready to receive and experience help. As worry arises remind yourself that you have surrendered the situation to God and that help is on its way, then be open to witnessing and experiencing God's grace.

CHAPTER 3

— ❧ —

All On My Own

As SOON AS I moved out of the home that I shared with my husband, a working relationship of mine became increasingly flirtatious. It didn't take long for things to escalate, and text messages moved from highly suggestive to blatant sexting.

One day he picked me up for lunch, and the moment I got in to the car we were holding hands and immediately affectionate; the chemistry was palpable.

The level of attraction I had for him and how desired I felt by him was like being on a high; I couldn't get enough, and I wanted more and more. I couldn't remember the last time I had felt like that, and after the tough decision I had just made and all the pain and tears, I welcomed in this lust and fire with open arms.

Like a drug, this sexual desire alleviated and allowed me to escape from the exhaustion and heartbreak that rested so heavily on me.

In a matter of weeks, I had gone from feeling unfulfilled and mediocre to feeling heartbroken and then uncertain, to now feeling desired and full of passion. There was just one problem. This man (lovingly referred to as Cargo Guy) had baggage — cargo, if you will — in the form of a long-term girlfriend.

We openly discussed our feelings and attraction for each other and both agreed that our chemistry was electric. Beyond the obvious physical attraction, it was easy for us to spend hours on the phone and discuss a wide range of topics. He shared personal and intimate things about himself and his life with me and I shared the same with him.

One evening over the phone we were talking about the future. We discussed everything from children to our careers and even had a laugh about how we met and how we had to keep our 'fling' from getting out around the office.

He then said, "Well it's a good story to tell the grandkids."

I paused, loving what he said but not knowing how to respond. He asked if I liked what he had said, and I responded with "Yes."

To which he said, "Well I like saying it."

During one of our secret, intimate "get togethers," we discussed our feelings for each other. That was when I asked about his current relationship, to which he responded that they would have to break up. I felt good hearing this, feeling as though there really was something between us, that he felt something for me and that maybe I was getting the relationship I had craved for so long.

Although I loved the way he made me feel and the way I felt about him, I knew this was wrong. I was enraptured by the lust, which was a distraction from the choice I had made and the intention I had set to choose what is right and best for me and to never settle. This was a test and Cargo Guy was a great teacher.

After speaking to my therapist, I sent Cargo Guy an email saying that I was putting our "relationship" on hold until we were both clear. I told him that I was clear: I was single and desired a relationship with him. He needed to get clear, too, before things continued, and he agreed.

As months went on, I didn't hear from him and our interactions at work stayed very formal. I secretly hoped that I would get a call or a text message from him saying he was single and ready to be with me. It never came, and I was disappointed in him for making the suggestion that we would one day be a couple and even more disappointed in myself in believing it would actually happen.

I realized that to have the feelings of passion, desire and fire that I so craved, they couldn't come from something or someone external. I knew that if I wanted this feeling of aliveness, then I would have to do the personal work on and for myself. I knew the journey wouldn't be quick or easy, but by taking the journey alone it would provide me with the discovery and feelings of aliveness that weren't dependent upon an external source.

Being the 'other woman' remains one of my greatest regrets, and I often asked myself "Is this the story I want to tell?"

"Is this the woman I want to be and the example I want to set?"

The answer was no, being the other woman was not something that I wanted to be a part of my story.

So there I was alone, as I needed to be, ready to embark on my own unchartered path.

All On My Own Exercise
Theme: Distractions & Addictions

———— ✑ ————

CARGO GUY WAS my distraction — a distraction from the enormity of the change I was facing. I wanted to feel comforted because I was in the vulnerable situation of my entire life being turned upside down. The desire and pleasure that came along with this fling was a welcome distraction, almost drug-like, as it completely masked the pain I was facing. As I've learnt, distractions are very similar to addictions. Both distractions and addictions keep us down and away from facing (and feeling) reality and moving forward in a new direction. I had to let Cargo Guy go, face the reality of my current life and move forward alone if I was really going to have the life that was calling me.

The following exercises will help you activate your awareness around what distractions and addictions you have that are holding you back. When answering the following questions, think, 'what are the reasons/excuses I use the most when I turn down or say no to doing something?', 'What are my most common excuses?'.

1. What is distracting you from the call upon your life? What is the thing you seem to always have to do that keeps you in routine? *Know that this book came into your life for a reason.
2. How are you avoiding the call upon your life?
3. What are you addicted to? (alcohol, drugs, food, sex, people, relationships, etc.)

4. List three examples within the last two weeks where you were guilty of 'glorifying busy'? When did you say or act as though you were so busy but really could have said yes to something new?
5. How do you really **feel** about your life?

Take Action!

Now that you have the awareness of what is keeping you away from choosing another way, it's time to take action. Remember that in order to step into a new life and way of being, a new choice must be taken.

So here is your homework: do something out of routine, sending a message to the Universe that you are no longer operating in the same, mundane sort of way. Over the next week do something new everyday, big or small. Go out for lunch with your co-workers, say yes to getting together with a friend in the evening, go to the gym, do yoga and/or attend a meditation class. Do something new, completely out of routine that feels good and feeds your soul. Even have a bit of fun with it. Do you always take the same route to work? Try a different way. Always order the same thing? Try something completely new, just get the energy flowing in a new and different direction and have fun!!!

CHAPTER 4

— ✿ —

Answering The Call

IT HAD BEEN three weeks since I left my husband, and I was wrapped up in an affair that was immediately gratifying and lustful.

One day after work as I was sitting in my car in the office parking lot talking dirty with Cargo Guy, my (soon to be) ex-husband called me. I ignored it, thinking he possibly wanted to discuss an offer on the house, and figured I'd call him back later. As I carried on my conversation, my ex called me again and again but I continued to ignored it. Then my grandparents called me.

"How random?" I thought, but I ignored their phone call, too. Finally, Cargo Guy and I reluctantly said good-bye, and I drove off from the parking lot and headed to the gym.

On the way to the gym, my ex called me again, and I decided to answer. He asked if my grandparents had reached me. I told him no and asked what was going on. "Pull over," he said, and my heart sank. I immediately thought that maybe my grandmother had been in a car accident.

I pulled over on the side of the road, put my car in park and asked him again what was going on. He answered by starting with an "I can't believe I have to tell you this," and then he told me that my seventeen year old brother, Nicholas, had killed himself.

I was hit by shock, and the impact was something I had never felt before; it hit me hard and in my chest and then began to push me down.

"No!" I screamed and continued to scream in my car as people walking by looked strangely at me. In my shock, I gave my ex a brief description of where I was and asked him to come get me.

I sat in my car alone surrounded by trauma and immersed in shock. I said to myself over and over again "No, my life doesn't look like this, no, my life won't be moving forward like this."

I wasn't going to accept this or allow this to be my experience; I was in total resistance to this now being my reality.

This news changed me and my life forever. The trauma and denial of my brother's news was pulling me down to an ugly place, a place I could have stayed forever. I felt myself spiraling down, but just as that was happening, a miracle happened.

A presence appeared that halted my spiraling, paused my hysteria, and grabbed my full attention. I looked to my right and nothing was technically "there," but I could feel it so strongly it was as though I could see it clear as day. I received the message loud and clear.

"You're going to be ok." I believed it. This message saved me.

I don't know how long I sat there and stared, but once I received this message, I returned to the stress of my currently reality.

I called my grandparents. "What the hell is going on?" I screamed.

He told me Nicholas was dead, and I screamed as he passed the phone to my grandmother. In my shock I asked my grandmother "Why?"

In her shock she told me "I don't know." My grandmother was the one who found him.

I then asked if my mom knew and my grandmother said no. Immediately I knew that I would have to tell her that her youngest child was dead. I told my grandmother that my ex was coming to get me and hung up the phone.

My ex arrived, and I opened the door still paralyzed in shock and he looked at me. Never in our nearly seven years together had he ever seen me like this, and he stood there not knowing what to do. Then he leaned in and hugged me. He got in my car and drove me back to his place, where I called my mom.

That moment is one I will never forget, and it is traumatizing even now for me to remember. My mother, living overseas at the time, flew back home immediately. That day, the day my brother was found, was also my other brother John's birthday, so that was a phone called that would have to wait to the next morning. I called my very good friend, Taren, and told her what happened, and she immediately came to get me.

I booked a flight for the next morning. That night I made many phone calls to family and friends regarding Nicholas. Hearing the reactions and shock from others was crippling. I was exhausted and drained.

Taren contacted a few friends, including Cargo Guy, to let them know what had happened. I went to bed. Unable to sleep, I laid there in disbelief that my little brother was gone. I received a text message from Cargo Guy expressing his condolences and reaching out should I need support. He then called me and we spoke over the phone. I told him everything that happened, I cried on the phone and he cried along with me. He asked if there was anything he could do and I asked for his help in booking my brother's flight back.

The next morning Taren took me to the airport. On my way there I called a friend of my brother John's to go be with him after I delivered the news. I asked his friend to take him to the airport, since he was going to have to travel across the country. As Taren drove in circles around the airport, I called my brother John. I told him our mom was on her way back to Canada and that he was going to have to get on a flight back home right away because Nicholas had killed himself. He was shocked and then broke down in tears. I began to cry and so did Taren. I told John I had to catch my flight and that Cargo Guy would call him with his flight details. I reminded him that he needed to get to the airport right away. Taren then dropped me off and left me with a big hug.

I was the first to arrive. John landed safely shortly thereafter, and more family and friends were gathering as well. When my mother's plane landed, we were waiting. As the elevator doors opened, she came out in a wheelchair and we all ran to hug her.

We were shaken, traumatized and forever changed.

Even amongst the chaos, shock and heartbreak, my faith knew this was a catalyst for something; there was a great reason for this even though I hated the fact that my brother was gone. This was the ultimate wake-up call and even though I was in pain, my experience in the car with the divine message I had received stayed with me as a constant reminder that I was going to be ok.

Everything was going to be ok.

Once we were all together, I found myself slipping into the old familiar patterns of taking care of everyone else and ensuring everything and everyone had what they needed.

I was playing mediator and caretaker, an all-too-familiar role. I kept busy making sure my mom was ok, calling friends and asking them to bring things to the house, arranging visits, and speaking with the coroner and funeral home. My own grief was placed on the back burner.

My mother, brother John and my brother's dad (my stepdad) and I arranged Nicholas' funeral. It was hell, not to mention that the four of us hadn't all been in the same room together for years. Our dysfunctional family dynamics were rising up to the surface. Immediately after we finished planning the funeral, we all left to go to the police station and read Nicholas' suicide note.

The four of us all sat in a room together, grief-stricken, exhausted and drained as the police officer came in holding a white piece of paper. I read the note first. It was full of darkness. It was awful and most of all it was not my brother, not the Nicholas I knew and loved. The rest of my family read it, and we were all in shock, crying, and in agreement that this was not our Nicholas.

Let me be clear, I am not suggesting nor do I think my brother's death was caused by anything other than suicide. What I mean is that who he was in that moment, that brief moment that was long enough for him to make the decision that he did, was not the Nicholas we all knew and loved. He was in a dark place, a state of mind that came over him and allowed him to take his own life.

After we left the police station it was as though we couldn't take any more. The drive back to our hotel was tense, as emotions were in full swing. Arguments started. As we parked, everyone got out of the car except for my mother, who answered a phone call. My brother came over to me, angry with his dad. My mother waved at us to stop talking, but we all proceeded to argue until my mother got out of the car and walked toward my stepdad, her ex-husband. My brother and I followed her, knowing that something was up.

My stepdad had tears in his eyes. I had seen him cry throughout the past few days, but this was a different type of crying and tears.

He looked at me, shaking, and said, "Look what I found."

He showed me two white rocks he had found amongst the section of grey rocks that surrounded the landscape of the hotel parking lot; one rock said "love" and the other said "courage," both in black printed writing.

The energy around us was different; we could all feel it and we were paralyzed and in awe as to what had just happened. We all began to cry, and my brother picked up my mother and carried her in to the hotel, and my stepfather and I quickly followed.

The second we all got in the hotel room, we sat on the bed in a circle with both the rocks in the middle.

I remember my mom so clearly stating, "This is my boy."

We all agreed, this was the Nicholas we knew, and this was his message. Another miracle had occurred in that moment, for me and this time for my family as well, right when we needed it most.

The following days, including the funeral, were hell, but the message from my brother was profound and stayed with me.

This message changed me and how I viewed things moving forward. My brother's death was a catalyst. It was the ultimate wake-up call to transform me and the life I was living. It was time for me to step out of mediocrity, to stop settling, and to break old patterns and beliefs. I chose to rise up to the challenge and not let my brother's death be in vain; what if I said no and continued to live a mundane life that I wasn't happy with? My brother's death then wouldn't have served a purpose, and I couldn't let that happen.

This message was clear and resonated through my entire body. I was being guided by a great power to something, but I didn't know what it was or what it would look like.

Once I got back home and the funeral was behind me, I made a vow to answer this call and to trust and do whatever was in the highest good.

I looked at my life honestly and made some decisions. I said good-bye to Cargo Guy. I got my own apartment and sent a big "Bring It On" message and intention out into the Universe about how I was ready for whatever it had in store for me.

The call had been answered, and I waited for the ride to begin.

Answering The Call Exercise
Theme: Choice

JUST WHEN I thought that I couldn't experience any more change, my little brother, my favourite person in the entire world, was gone. Hearing that news made it easy to fall into a dark place, never to come out. However, something came in and saved me, and although coming back to my reality wasn't easy, the message of 'you're going to be ok' stayed with me. My brother's death was a call for transformation. Nicholas' message of 'love and courage' was clear, and I was going to need both should I make the choice to answer this call and take my life in a completely different direction. It was time, time for radical change, and if I was going to do that I was going to have to make new choices.

The following exercises will help you activate awareness of your patterns around choice. When answering the following questions think, feel and intend to look at the core truth around your relationship with choice. Get to a quiet space and make a commitment to yourself and to God to be fully honest when answering.

1. What are your patterns around choice? Do you continually make the same choices? Do you give up, or avoid making choices (self-sabotage)? Do you embrace change?
2. What is OK in your life right now, meaning what are you happy and content with? What is working well for you in regards to the issue you are facing?

3. What is **not** OK in your life right now, what feels 'off' for you? What isn't working well for you in regards to the issue you are facing?
4. Beyond all the things you believe you should do or what your family or others believe you should do, What is best for **you**? What do you know to be best for you?
5. Are you willing to make another choice?
6. What is your new choice?

*Remember choice is a catalyst! "If you want to change your life, you must change your choices." - Dianne Tharp

Take Action!

Now that you are fully aware of your relationship to choice and what needs to change in your life, it's time to take action. Again, this book came into your life for a reason, so trust that it's ok and that it's time to choose a new way of living and being. Complete joy and alignment awaits.

Here is your homework: make a choice. Big or small, or both. Look at what isn't working in your life and examine how you can choose a different way to interact with this situation. If you're struggling with how you can approach it differently ask yourself 'If I did know how to approach/interact with this what would that look like'? Be awake, attentive and conscious as you move forward and make this new choice. It may feel awkward and clumsy because it's your first time stepping out of set ways; it is the newness of the new way that makes you feel a bit wobbly.

*Remember the exercise from Chapter 1: know you can trust yourself and know that there is a greater power at work here that has your highest interest in mind at all times. You got this!!!

CHAPTER 5

— ✂ —

The Spiritual Anchor

THERAPY: I AM a big fan and always have been. As you can imagine, with the emotional storm that was raging in my life, I went looking for psychological help.

I have known a beautiful and wise woman for years to whom I've occasionally gone to for sessions. With everything I had recently experienced, I chose to see her again, this time more frequently.

I had had a session with her after I left my husband but before the death of my brother. Her ability to hold space allowed my own inner truth and knowing to present itself in a way that silenced my mind.

These sessions were and are critical to my being able to move forward in a healthy way, in a way where I was processing through all that had occurred rather than suppressing and not dealing with what had transpired in my life.

My therapist gave me some critical tools continue to serve me along my journey. I reference them prior to making any decisions or moving forward. The tools consist of my spiritual principles, my values and my core desired feelings.

*All the times I've gone off track were because I didn't look to see if whatever choice I was making was in alignment with my spiritual principles and values and if it was going to bring me my desired feelings.

Spiritual principles: The three things that I <u>do</u> that make an impact in the world. They are how I leave my imprint with everything and everyone I meet.

Every day I must practice and behave in a way that is in alignment with my spiritual principles. These guides ensure that I am staying true to myself when making decisions on what I do and who I spend my time with. If there is a person or opportunity that contradicts my spiritual principles, then I know that that situation does not serve me or the highest good.

My spiritual principles:

- There is one ultimate, all-connecting Source
- There is great value and importance in the divine feminine
- I am light, leading the way

Values: They are my internal, personal standards. How am I going to choose to behave in the world? What will I stand for? What is important to me?

These have been so important to me because anytime something or someone is operating in a way that goes against my values, I know that situation is not for me, and it's time for me to make a decision.

My personal values:

- Freedom
- Courage
- Commitment
- Compassion
- Evolution

Desired Feelings: When we pursue something in life, we aren't necessarily going after that particular situation, object or person; what we're really going after is the feeling we believe those things will bring us. Any time I need to make a decision about a job, a relationship or any significant or small move, I look to see if this choice will bring me all five of my desired feelings. If not, then I don't do it.

Anytime I have not referred to my desired feelings and made a decision that didn't bring me all five of them, I was left either upset or angry and I regretted the choice I made. However, it left me with another life lesson.

My cored desired feelings:

- Divinely Feminine
- Aligned
- Orgasmic
- Impactful
- Expansive

Having had these tools, these anchors, prior to my marriage and other decisions I made in my past could have saved me from a lot of pain, disappointment and regret. This is another life lesson I'm passing on so that maybe others don't have to learn the hard way.

The anchor formed by my spiritual principles, values and desired feelings is something I look at regularly to ensure that my choices and behavior are in alignment. Every time (and I mean every time) I have made a choice that was fully aligned with this anchor, it has served me in the most positive and fulfilling way.

Another thing that I found to be absolutely critical in my journey, along with my anchor, is support. It is important to have a place to fall, someone who cares but who is also honest and objective and can guide me with a loving intention. This has been instrumental in my continuing to say yes to the call made on my life. I can't do it alone, and whenever I get shaken up and wobbled in uncertainty, having someone there to remind me of my anchor, listen to my story, and be a steady source of wisdom provides me with unmeasurable support and gratitude.

My anchor is made up of principles, values and feelings, along with support, and that is what keeps me on my path as I move along in uncertainty. As I move into the unknown, unsure of where my next step will take me, I know that if I have my anchor and some form of support, I will be moving along in the right direction and all will be ok. It may still be scary, but I will be ok.

The Spiritual Anchor Exercise
Theme: Creating Your Own North Star

ॐ

THE CHOICE TO enter a new new life and way of being meant that I was going into unchartered water, and I needed something constant to go to that would help guide me through the unknown. I developed my values: Freedom, Evolution, Courage, Commitment and Compassion. I also developed my desired feelings: Divinely Feminine, Aligned, Orgasmic, Impactful and Expansive. My values and desired feelings make up a portion of my anchor (we'll develop the last piece in the next chapter) that makes sure I keep moving in the direction of what is true and right for me.

Since you've made the decision to break free of old patterns, you will need to develop your own anchor to help guide you through your new, unchartered water.

Values
Values are your inner measure of what is right and what is wrong for you. If your life isn't lining up with your values, then part of you is dying. If you are getting all your values from life then you are truly living.

Knowing your values is critical. If you don't know what you stand for then you'll fall for anything. It's important to know when developing your values that you'd live or die for your top three values.

Ask your self the following questions:

1. What do you stand for?
2. What are three things that if you didn't have them part (or all) of you would die?
3. During times of change or uncertainty what do you reference and use to guide your decisions?

It's crucial that you are clear on what **your** values are, as we are often conditioned by what our family or friends value, and we ignore what is true for us.

Feelings

When we are going after something, a new job, money, car, etc., we aren't actually going after the object but the feeling that we believe that object will bring.

Feelings let you know how you are doing. If you feel off then that means something needs to be realigned in your life. If you feel great then you know that you're in alignment with who you are and where you desire to be.

Ask yourself the following questions:

1. When you envision yourself as successful (what ever success looks like for you) what feeling, beyond feeling successful, does that bring you?
2. What is something you love doing or when was a time you felt your best? What were you feeling in that moment?
3. Think back to when you were 10 years old, what were you interested in? What were you playing with? How did doing that thing make you feel?

4. What is a feeling that you do not like to experience and feel? Often times knowing what we don't like and looking at the opposite feeling can give us some insights.

Take Action!

Now it is time to discover your values and desired feelings and begin to develop your anchor. It can be very helpful to work with a therapist to develop these; this helps to ensure you become aware of your values and feelings and not those that perhaps your family and friends have told you that you should have.

Below are some suggested resources to help you to develop your values and desired feelings.

Values:

Article #1: Define your personal core values
Article #2: Finding your core values in five easy steps
Therapist: Dianne Tharp can take you through the process of discovering your top five values

Desired Feelings:

Book: The Desire Map. Danielle Laporte is an expert in the area of developing your core desired feelings
Therapist: Dianne Tharp can take you through the process of discovering your top five desired feelings
Once you have your top five values and desired feelings, use them! They will be instrumental in guiding you through changes and choice points that you will inevitably face. Write them down, carry them in your wallet, post them in your office, see them, use them and experience their guidance.

CHAPTER 6

Spiritual Immersion

AFTER ALL THAT I'd been through and the personal work and healing I had done, I knew without a doubt there was a reason that all this was happening in my life. Even though it was painful and difficult, it felt like it was all part of a bigger plan.

Since I knew there was something divine at work in my life, I decided to delve deeper into my spirituality. My therapist lived in Ubud, Bali, and was holding a retreat. I didn't exactly know the details, but I felt called to go, and I trusted her and the work she does.

I arrived in Ubud, the spiritual hub of Bali, and just being there, amongst that energy, soothed me and put me at ease. I had no idea what to expect from Bali or the retreat, so I arrived completely open and without any need to know what was in store.

On day one, the group got together, and our first question was "What's your relationship like with your mother?"

My immediate (and out loud) response was: "Wow, you don't waste any time do you?"

I knew at that point we were all in for it. We visited various sacred sites and were guided through different therapies by my therapist. One ancient healer, who I was especially touched by, had people sit in front of him while he touched specific pressure points on their face and head that would indicate to him what was off either physically or emotionally. He then had them lie down while he took a wand and hit certain points on the toes of the left foot. There were pressure points that he hit that made many people, myself included, scream.

When my turn came up, I was excited to see what he would pick up on. I was immediately drawn to him. He sat me down in front of him and touched certain points on my face and head and then he hit a spot on my head that was so painful I jumped.

"Too much thinking." he said.

You have no idea, I thought to myself. Then I lay down in front of him, and with his wand he began to press the pressure points on my toes. He pressed on one spot, then another, and then the motherload. Good god did that hurt. I initially thought I might have levitated off the ground. I looked at him and he, ever so compassionately, put his hand on my leg and said, "You need a new heart."

I began to cry and he looked over at my therapist, asked her a few questions, and she nodded. I told him about my divorce and the death of my brother and I felt his compassion for me in a way that truly touched me.

He proceeded to give me a new heart, which entailed his drawing sacred geometry and patterns on my chest. He also stood over me, said a prayer, and did some energy work. I thanked him, and he told me, regarding my heart, "Next time be more careful."

Once I was done, my fellow participants had their time with him, and I witnessed miracles occur over and over again, everything from energy shifts to the healing of physical ailments. I had to take a moment and let all that I was seeing and experiencing really settle in. I mean, I believed in the stuff but to bear witness to it was incredible and I was in awe.

The week was filled with powerful experiences, with another one being a visit to an awakened being. Ida Resi Alit was awakened when she was twenty; she died twice and woke up speaking twelve languages, including fluent Sanskrit. We arrived, in full traditional Balinese ceremony attire, as she was giving water purification to the people before us. As I sat there and watched people, two at a time, stand before her and receive their water purification, I saw that something was occurring; everyone's reactions were explosive, highly charged, as if a purging was happening. As one extremely shy, quiet and reserved woman in our group had the water poured over her, she began to yell and scream and it was as though she had given herself permission to let the rage and anger out.

When it was my turn, I approached nervously, unsure what I was going to experience. As I neared the altar where she was kneeling, my heart began to vibrate in a way that I'd never experienced before, and I began to weep. I wondered what was happening to me, but I stood there and continued to cry while she chanted and poured water over my head. She told me to yell out and stomp my feet and I followed her directions. When she was finished, I moved away from her altar, stood on the ground, and felt the sun over me. I wasn't sure what had just happened to me.

I changed into dry clothes, and a large group of us all sat together as Ida came over and guided us through a meditation.

The entire week was filled with divine therapies that, upon reflection, I can see changed me at a deep, cellular level. We did yoga, talk therapy and breathwork, and had a tantrum session in the pool, along with the visits to sacred sites, traditional healers, and holy women.

On our last night, we were asked to share with everyone what we believed this experience had brought us and how it had changed us. I didn't know the answer in that moment, as it all was a lot to digest, but I did express my gratitude. After all I had experienced, I knew something bigger than me was at work in my life. I expressed my gratitude to the universal power that thought that perhaps there was something within me deserving of expression and sharing with the world.

This retreat intended to deliver "tangible experiences of the divine," and it did exactly that. In many ways, this retreat was a turning point in itself. After witnessing and having such mystical and Godly encounters, I could never return to living my life the same way. The energetic bar had been raised, and now it was up to me to discover a new life that was aligned with my newly awakened, authentic and higher self.

Spiritual Immersion Exercise
Theme: Spirituality

— ❧ —

HAVING SUCH DIVINE experiences really had me examine who I was at the core of my being. Who was I? What was I a piece of? Where did I come from? What was I here to do? These questions had me look beyond my human experience and really ask what I was all about. If my life was going to feel meaningful, what would I be doing with my life? What would I be willing to fight for? What influence did I desire to have on the world?

In this exercise we are going to develop your three spiritual principles and therefore complete your anchor. Spiritual principles are foundational; they are your external truth, like your own universal truth or law. They are much broader than your values and desired feelings. Think of them as the fuel to your fire because without them, 'what is the point?' These spiritual principles are the fuel to your vehicle of how you impact the world.

As an example, here are my spiritual principles:

- There is one ultimate, all connecting divine source
- There is great value and importance in the divine feminine
- I am light; leading the way

The descriptions below will help clarify the differences between spiritual principles, values and desired feelings:

Spiritual principles - These are your code of behaviour or ethics, your personal law by which you chose to abide. You might recommend that others follow it because it brings peace, love and respect and authentically creates inspiration in the world. Spiritual principles are more external, addressing how you behave and act in the world, with values being more internal.

Values - These are your standards of behaviour. They tell you how you meet your Spiritual Principles of being and living your own life. When you do not meet these self-set standards, you feel as though you are dying inside. Values are internal, your own personal ethics and standards, with spiritual principles being more external.

Desired Feelings - The feeling of being authentic, unique, divine and in complete alignment with God and your true self. Your desired feelings are the result of practicing your spiritual principles and living your values. Feeling or not feeling you desired feelings let you know how you are doing; they are your gauge.

Here are some questions to ask yourself to help reveal your spiritual principles:

1. What are you devoted to?
2. What issue(s) get you all fired up?
3. What do you stick up and fight for?
4. How do you want to impact the world?
5. What change would you like to evoke?
6. What external beliefs do you hold that if they turned out not to be true would be completely deflating, disappointing and sad?

Take Action!

Now is the time to complete your anchor and discover and align yourself to your spiritual principles. Once you have answered the above questions, it is very common to not have complete clarity about your spiritual principles. It is my recommendation that you work with someone to help really nail down your spiritual principles.

For someone to work with, I recommend <u>Dianne Tharp</u>. She is an expert in this area and can help you to determine your spiritual principles along with your values and desired feelings.

Once you have your spiritual principles, write them down along with your values and desired feelings and put them up somewhere to ensure you see them on a daily basis. You may even keep a copy in your wallet as a constant reminder and a tool to keep you in alignment.

CHAPTER 7

---- ❦ ----

Boundaries

WHILE IN BALI, having a tangible experience of the divine, I met up with a man whom I had done some personal coaching sessions with. He was a highly intuitive healer - let's call him Healer Man. Once we had had a few sessions, and I moved through some pretty heavy stuff, a bit of a friendship started to develop. We got along really well and had the same sense of humor, so when I arrived in Bali (where he lived) we planned to meet up.

I got to the island just over a week prior to the retreat start, which gave me time to spend with friends, Healer Man and my mother, who had now moved to Bali following my brother's death. For our first meeting, I had planned a group dinner, and when my friends saw me with Healer Man, our friendship and chemistry was obvious.

One evening Healer Man and I went out just the two of us. He took me to a restaurant and then we ended up at a jazz club. After talking and getting closer throughout the evening, we kissed. We spent that night together, and so began the week of our whirlwind romance, which we tried to hide from everyone, unsuccessfully.

By the time I began the retreat, our romance was out in the open. We weren't able to see each other for that week, but once the retreat ended, we reunited and spent my last night in Bali together. Things were moving quickly, and I could tell he cared for me deeply. In that whirlwind of a week "I love you's" were shared.

Although I was no doubt smitten, it also felt a bit too quick for me. However, it was all so wonderful that I kept going along with it.

Since Healer Man's work allowed him to work anywhere, he decided to come over to Canada. So, after a few weeks of being apart, Healer Man flew from Bali to Canada (as my boyfriend) and moved into my apartment with me. Since we hadn't seen each other for a while, the first few weeks were great, but shortly after that things started to wobble. We lived together in my small, one-bedroom, downtown apartment. It was a very different look compared to a bungalow in Bali.

Everyone around me was so excited for me, and it did sound like quite the fairytale. After experiencing divorce and death, I went to Bali, fell and love, and the man followed me back to Canada. However, it was a bit too much too fast, to say the least. We argued; what he wanted and what I wanted were completely different. There was no friendship foundation to our relationship. If I were to have been honest with myself, it was probably not the time to start a romance. It was just eight months since I left my husband and just over 7 months since my brother's death. I was still in a space where I was healing.

Healer Man and I were on the same page regarding our relationship; it needed to end, and it did. However, we did still care for each other deeply, and after we ended our relationship, a beautiful soulmate friendship developed. Over the next few months, I continued to help and support him around his work by organizing various evenings, sessions and workshops.

We had become best friends; we spent all our time together and told each other everything. I was grateful for having a like-minded friend in my life whom I could (and did) share everything with.

I put Healer Man up on a bit of a pedestal. His spiritual abilities and beliefs were something I admired, and he had great charisma that I was blinded by. Blinded in a way where I would question, doubt and/or disre-gard my own inner knowing, buying in to the idea that he knew more than me. When Healer Man would offer suggestions on what to do and how to do it, I chose to ignore my own approach and gut instinct, and I allowed myself to be overly and easily influenced by him.

Lines were very blurred as we remained friends after our break up. We continued to sleep together for a month after we broke up and even after that we spent all our free time together and were very affectionate. Should you have seen us you would have thought we were still together. I allowed myself to get wrapped up in this. After we ended our romantic relationship, I completely expected a clear line to be drawn, but as the affection remained I felt bad about turning it down even though I knew the line in the sand needed to be drawn. Our being friends needed to be just that, friends.

As our friendship continued, I had a difficult time saying no to him and would take on and accept all his suggestions even when I knew that they didn't work for me and I should have been saying no. I was exhausted, emotionally eating, gaining weight and putting my needs and desires off to the side.

At the same time, I was exploring and organizing my next move (that story is coming a bit later). However, Healer Man asked me to leave my job earlier than planned to come and work for him. Without referring to my anchor, I agreed. So for my last six weeks in Canada, I worked for Healer Man. He had gone from therapist, to lover, friend, and now, my boss.

The six weeks we worked together, which were my last in Canada, started out fine but quickly went downhill, much like our relationship. There were a lot of things that should have been clarified first. From my perspective, the expectations were unrealistic and the direction unclear.

My last few weeks in Canada were hell; I was working long hours and putting his work before spending my last moments with my friends who I would soon be leaving for an unknown amount of time. Tensions were high and too frequently taken out on me, and I slipped into the pattern of not saying anything.

There was a set end date, and when that day came I was relieved, yet I still hadn't spoken my truth and established boundaries and standards for myself.

Upon reflection, this period of my life and how I handled it brings up disappointment, mostly in myself, especially since I knew better. Healer Man was a great teacher, and one of the main things I learned was that we do not have to accept the entirety of someone's teachings. Healer Man did have great teachings and advice, but knowing what I know now, I didn't have to take the entire lesson. I could have taken pieces and used them in a way that best worked for me.

If I could give a piece of advice to myself it would be to reflect, when being given advice: what is perhaps a projection and maybe not something that would serve me?

Speaking my truth and saying no is another big lesson. I compromised way too much in this relationship, which broke the commitment I made to myself to follow what is best and true for me and to never settle. My reasoning for not wanting to speak out was that I didn't want to hurt someone, but I ended up sacrificing myself. By the time our work arrangement was done I was drained, my self-esteem was diminished, and I had gained a significant amount of weight. I looked and felt like someone who hadn't taken care of themselves (and I hadn't). Worst of all, I knew better.

Boundaries Exercise
Theme: Boundaries

— ℘ —

HEALER MAN'S PRESENCE in my life felt divinely placed; through good times and bad he was a great teacher. He opened my eyes to many wonderful new possibilities, but he also tested me, my standards, my self worth and what I stood for.

This relationship reminded me of my spiritual principles, values and desired feelings and how quickly I can find yourself out of alignment when I ignore them. I learned how critical it was to first be loyal to myself.

For this exercise we are going to develop some awareness around what you are currently doing in your life that is not working and not aligned with who you are, what you stand for and how you want to feel. Take the time you need to centre yourself and intend to answer the following questions truthfully:

1. Where are you saying Yes in your life when you know you should be saying No?
2. Where are you saying No in your life when you know you should be saying Yes?

Take Action!
Begin to follow your knowing. Your homework is to say No to at least one (if not all) of the things you listed above where you have been saying Yes.

In addition, you must say Yes to at least one (if not all) of the things you listed above where you have been saying No.

This is a simple but powerful (and vulnerable) exercise. Be kind with yourself as you begin to do things in a different way and know that you'll be a bit clumsy, but that is OK. Acknowledge that you are taking some courageous steps. Give yourself some credit!

CHAPTER 8

Releasing the Old

I CRAVED A new life, and I craved adventure. I looked around at my life, and I knew it wasn't what I wanted. I sat in my own apartment, my own space completely furnished with nice things and went to a job that I could do without any real effort. I wanted more and I knew I was being called.

I started exploring what my next step could be; I applied for an Australian work visa and was approved almost immediately. I was excited about working abroad, and I initially thought I would leave straight to Australia to begin work. As I thought about things more in depth, I discovered I needed time after everything I had been through in the past year. I needed to focus solely on me and no one else. I asked myself what that looked like, but I didn't fully know. All I knew was that I wanted to travel.

Before I could create, develop and embark on a spiritual journey, I had to leave my old life behind. Although I knew it wasn't the life I wanted, letting it all go before knowing my next step and not knowing if my next step would pay off was terrifying.

I looked around my apartment and saw so much stuff and so many reasons not to go. I had furniture, electronics, kitchen appliances, and more clothes than my poor closet could hold. What would I come back to should I need to? What would be waiting here for me should this journey fail, should I fail?

If I was going to travel abroad I would need two suitcases. I would need one to ship to Australia for when I arrived and the other to bring with me. How could I get everything I needed in to two suitcases?

I began to panic and doubt myself.

"What the hell am I doing?" I thought out loud.

But the idea of staying, continuing to live the routine, a day in and day out life, was more painful for me than the unknown.

So I began my letting go of the items that were keeping me in my old life. I gave away bags of clothes to a charity and sold all my furniture and everything in my kitchen to the woman who was moving into my apartment after me. My grandmother even bought my car. There I was all of a sudden no longer with the 'security' of my things, but also unburdened by them.

I was ready for the next phase. I had just sent the Universe a big message saying that I was ready and willing for a new life and open to receive the gifts and lessons along the journey.

So I did it! I sold everything and found myself spending my last month in Canada living in my friend's basement with everything I owned (apart from 2 boxes in storage) fitting into two suitcases. Even amongst my fear, I knew I no longer wanted the status quo there was even a trace of excitement and eagerness about what I was going to experience, who I was going to meet and what I was going to discover about myself.

Releasing the Old Exercise
Theme: Giving Up Attachments

———— ♋ ————

I HAD GOTTEN rid of everything, and I was terrified. I was approaching 30, and I now only had two suitcases to my name; this was the opposite thing to be doing according to social standards. I was without the perceived security of my things, my apartment, car, clothes, etc., and even though I had the thoughts of 'what have I done?' and 'what if I fall, what will I come back to?' I felt unburdened by them and free to move forward without anything holding me back.

In this exercise you are going to take an honest look at what you are attached to and what programming you are under that may no longer serve who you are and where you desire to be.

Take a moment to relax, still your mind and intend to answer these questions honestly, from the truth of who you are:

1. What are you attached to?
    A. What things are you attached to? (Any material objects such as a home, car, clothing etc)
    B. What beliefs are you attached to?
    C. What people or relationships are you attached to?
    D. What labels are you attached to? (Are you the caregiver, good girl, saviour etc)

2. Are any of these holding you back from moving forward in your desired direction or preventing you from becoming who you desire to be? How so?

3. Without these attachments and labels who are you free to become? What does your life look like and how do you feel without these? Be specific.

Take Action!

Take a moment to examine what you wrote above. What are the main things holding you back? How can you begin to shift your attachment and let them go? If you are unable to let them go entirely, what can change within them? For example, you may be a mother and feel as though your responsibility to your children is limiting you from fully stepping in to a new life. What changes can you make? Are you able to ask for help? Do you need to go to every after school activity? Where can you begin to fit in your own desires? Remember whatever is in your highest good is in the highest good of all. Put yourself on the priority list and be kind to yourself!

CHAPTER 9

※

Creating the Adventure

I CONTINUED TO crave adventure and a new life and I was ready to leave my old world behind. I knew I would land in Australia at some point and begin to work, but first I needed a break.

My divorce left me with the money I had collected while I was saving for a down payment for the house we bought, which left me with the freedom to take some time off.

I knew I wanted to travel; I love the idea of being somewhere I've never been before, somewhere completely different. I was privileged enough to have five months to fill with whatever locations and activities that called me until I had to be in Australia.

I began by looking at my interests and asking myself what I was continually drawn to. I can't walk by a spiritual bookstore without going in, and I am obsessed with my own spiritual growth and development. So, I knew spirituality and my desire to connect to the Universe would be the main drivers in planning my journey.

I thought about meditation, yoga and even going back to Bali. I spoke to Healer Man about it, and he shared some of his own journey with me. He'd been on a ten day vipassana silent retreat and spent time in Thailand doing yoga. I did my research and found myself drawn to do ten days of meditation. When I do something, it's pretty much to the theme of "go hard or go home," and this would be exactly that. Ten days of meditation, ten hours per day, no speaking, reading, or writing and not even any eye contact with anyone: I was in! I wanted to connect, tap into that infinite place, to God, and I felt these ten days could help me do it.

I continued my research and looked into a yoga school in Thailand that happened to be a tantric yoga school - I was intrigued. I wouldn't ever describe myself as a sexually expressive person. I liked sex, don't get me wrong, and I knew that at times it could be really fun. I had just been in a long-term monogamous relationship, and as those in relationships know, the burning fire of desire starts to dwindle after a while. Prior to that, I had had a few interactions with men but nothing especially mind-blowing. I realized that I had never really explored my sexuality at all; I rarely paid attention to my own sexual desires and couldn't tell you the last time I masturbated.

I began to really sit with this and was reminded of conversations with friends who would talk about being able to make themselves orgasm when they were four years old! I was shocked at their stories; I wasn't able to orgasm in my late twenties without the help of a high speed vibrator that was only (and rarely) used to give me a fleeting clitoral orgasm.

I had never really and fully experienced sex in a way that many describe and was unsure if it was even possible for me to experience an orgasm. As I would come to understand later, I was sexually suppressed and totally naive.

At the tantric yoga school in Thailand, along with yoga, they offered a few tantra courses. Tantra is a holistic spiritual path that recognizes both the spiritual and the material as pathways to the divine. Since tantra is holistic, it couldn't have left sex out. So, in the spirit of my "go hard or go home" mentality, I registered.

Healer Man was planning to return to Bali shortly after I left Canada to lead one of his spiritual retreats and asked me to help out. Knowing the beauty and magic of Bali, I without hesitation agreed.

So my trip started to come together. I decided to kick off my journey with the ten day silent retreat just outside of Kuala Lumpur, Malaysia, followed by some time in Bali, seeing my mother and friends and attending Healer Man's spiritual retreat. That would then be followed by three months in Thailand where I would be immersed in yoga, meditation and tantra.

Serendipitously during this time my biological father and I had started communicating via email. About three years prior to this I had contacted him out of the blue via Facebook, and a little while after that we met and started to communicate more frequently. We were slowly beginning to develop a relationship. I shared with him my plan to travel around before heading over and settling in Australia, and he invited me to come visit him in his Macau, China, where he lived. At that point, we had only met face-to-face three times in my entire life. I had met his wife once and his two teen and preteen daughters didn't even know of my existence. I said yes to this invitation, amazed. Throughout my whole life there had been a hope and desire to get to know him, and now it was finally happening.

So my journey was planned: silent retreat in Malaysia, spiritual retreat in Bali, yoga, meditation and tantra in Thailand, followed by Chinese New Year with my dad and then a new adventure in Australia.

When I looked at my plans, I felt excited and eager to experience it all, which indicated to me that it was the right journey.

Creating The Adventure Exercise
Theme: Curiosity & Interest

———— ✂ ————

As I BEGAN to reflect on, research, and create my own adventure, I really allowed for this time to be all about me. I only thought about what I enjoyed and didn't allow the opinions and projects of others to influence or diminish my anticipation. When looking at how I wanted to fill up my adventure, I gave some real attention to what immediately came to mind. I spent time thinking about what I was most curious about and what I have always been interested in. I also noticed that when I put it out to the Universe that I wanted to go on my own spiritual journey of self-discovery, I met people who shared experiences I found interesting, I saw relevant advertisements, and I stumbled across helpful websites. Once the intention was out there, the Universe kept sending me messages.

For this exercise really allow your curious, creative and adventurous self come through as you create your own spiritual journey.

1. What are some things you would like to experience on this journey?
2. What have you always been interested in?
3. What do you desire to get out of this journey?
4. Who do you want to be at the end of this journey?
5. What is your ultimate intention for this journey? (For example mine was to experience who I am and to discover how I can serve)

6. What does this journey look like? (Be specific, where are you going? What specific things are you doing? Be your own travel agent)
7. How do you want to feel on this journey? Are all your desired feelings met?

Take Action!

Now that you know what your spiritual journey is, it's time to make it happen. Set specific goals and deadlines. When will you start the first piece of this journey? Whether you begin a workshop, class, trip or retreat, when is your specific start date? If you are unable to embark on your journey due to things like finances, look at what you desire to get out of your journey and ask yourself what can be done now, in order to give you the experience you are searching for. If you desire to do yoga, do you need to go across the world to do it? How can you express this interest within your current (but not permanent) reality?

Set goals and create a specific plan. When will you start? How much are you committing to save every month in order to really set out of this adventure that is calling you?

Remember that once you start this exercise the Universe will begin to send you messages, hints and guidance - look out for them and be ready to let them in. Allow these subtle cues to influence your path and have fun creating this exciting new adventure!

CHAPTER 10

Let the Spiritual Journey Begin...

"WELL IT'S STARTED," I said to myself in the back of a taxi as I drove through the tropical city of Kuala Lumpur, where I spent two days prior to starting my ten-day vipassana silent retreat.

As I entered the retreat centre, registration began, and we were given strict directions and guidelines. We were to participate in noble silence (complete silence) for ten days, with no distractions, which included no cell phones, laptops, iPads, music, books, pen or paper (which meant no journalling), and we were asked to refrain from eye contact. Once the directions were given, so began the ten days of noble silence.

We had a very strict schedule:

- 4 am: Wake up bell
- 4:30 - 6:30 am: Two hour morning meditation
- 6:30 - 8 am: Breakfast break
- 8 - 9am: Group Meditation in the hall
- 9 - 11am: Meditation in the hall or in your room
- 11 - 12 pm: Lunch Break
- 12 - 1pm: Rest and interviews with the teacher
- 1 - 2:30 pm: Meditate in the hall or in room
- 2:30 - 3:30 pm: Group Meditation in the hall
- 3:30 - 5 pm: Meditate in the hall or in room
- 5 - 6 pm: Tea break
- 6 - 7 pm: Group Meditation in the hall

- 7 - 8:15 pm: Teacher's discourse in the hall
- 8:15 - 9 pm: Group meditation in the hall
- 9 - 10 pm: Question time
- 10 pm: Lights out

I felt really ready for this and completely OK with the idea of disconnecting from society and not having my phone or laptop with me or even my journal. What I was most nervous about was the meditation and being alone with just me and my thoughts.

My first three days were hell and felt as if they were going to go on forever, I found myself looking at people who I knew this wasn't their first time doing the retreat.

I stared at them, irritated and wondering "Who volunteers to do this more than once?!" and "Why are you choosing to do this AGAIN?"

The thoughts running through my head were endless, and although we were told not to be hard on ourselves because we were having the thoughts, it was very difficult. I would start to beat myself up because I was having these random and erratic thoughts and then I began to beat myself up for beating myself up! It was endless.

During the first three days I experienced such exhaustion, and it had nothing to do with the jetlag. It was deep and heavy. I even found myself falling asleep (and drooling) during the teacher's discourse at the end of the evening.

In my frustration and panic that I was missing key opportunities and information, I went to go see the teacher. I told her about all my crazy thoughts, my extreme fatigue, and how I felt that I was missing and wasting a great opportunity because I kept having many thoughts and falling asleep. My teacher told me this was all normal and that there was an extreme fatigue within me and assured me that day four would be much better, but I wasn't as confident.

Well, my teacher was right. Days four and five were much better and calmer. Let me assure you, I had still had thoughts, but I was much nicer to myself about it and continued to bring myself back to observing my breath.

Just when I thought things were getting better (and naively thought they might stay that way), days six and seven were very challenging. It seemed as though I was going backwards; I had just had two good days and now my crazy and active thoughts had returned. I approached my teacher, yet again worried that I was not getting everything I could be out of this experience. She told me that these thoughts were coming up to be released, just like when you start to only eat healthy foods, your body goes through a detox. She said this practice is like a detox of the mind. She also mentioned that anything that happens from this point on is good and reminded me that these thoughts were releasing, and that made me feel much better.

I didn't miss the outside world, nor did I miss my laptop, cell phone or Facebook. Being removed from the rest of the world wasn't the hard part; it was the meditation I struggled with most.

On the eighth day I decided to meditate in my room versus in the hall and lay down on my bed (I broke the "don't lie down while you're meditating" rule), and I experienced a really beautiful meditation. I was fully present as I observed my own energy move from side to side and up and down through my whole body; I loved noticing and watching the energy move within myself. I felt really good.

Days nine and ten came and brought many thoughts with them. My mind was getting ahead of me planning where I would be going once the ten days were over, so I had to continually bring myself back to the present moment.

I believe it was on day nine when I was on a break and thought I would go for a walk around the grounds. Immediately after I left my room, I realized I was tired and went back. As soon as I lay down on my bed, fears about Australia crept in, and I burst in to tears. I was there alone, just me, my fears and tears. I let it out and allowed myself to finally feel the feelings I had locked away.

The moment I realized these feelings were okay and allowed them to be experienced, they moved on and left and I no longer felt the fear, sadness, or anxiety about my life six months down the line.

On day ten, noble silence was lifted quite early in the day. Once we had our final meditation, we were allowed to speak. In that moment, I found that I didn't want to. I felt comfortable and safe within the silence.

People began to talk outside the hall, which completely shifted the energy. The roller coaster of the ten days fascinated me. I went from thinking it was going to be a grueling, torturous ten days to having a magical meditation experience, to feeling warmth within the silence.

I returned to the world lighter and clearer, open and ready for Bali's magic!

When I arrived in Bali, I remembered how my first time there, not so long ago, I had attended my therapist's retreat that really changed me, and now I was getting the chance to help organize one that I hoped would do the same for others.

Before Healer Man arrived from Canada, I had a few days alone with my mother and friends, and I got the chance to connect with some beautiful, spiritual women that I know and love.

Once Healer Man arrived, I began putting together the final details of his retreat, and although I was getting excited about the activities and healers we were going to see during this retreat, our relationship was still a bit rocky. Working together proved to be something we just shouldn't do together.

During the retreat, Bali was magical, as always, and I watched traditional healers bestow their magic and gifts upon everyone. The retreat was powerful. Watching healings occur right in front of my eyes always reminds me that there is something bigger at work.

Things between Healer Man and I got a bit better once the retreat was over because my work with him ended and I was relieved. The past two weeks in Bali with him had been stressful and demanding. I was looking forward to having some separation between us as the countdown to Thailand began.

Healer Man went off to Kuala Lumpur for a few days, and since I was flying through I would see him there on my way to Thailand. This gave me a great chance to spend the last days in Bali with my mom. This time also gave me the chance to reflect on not only Bali and the silent retreat, but my relationship with Healer Man in general. I didn't want the relationship to continue on the way that it had the last few months, and I knew I needed to address it.

Once I landed in Kuala Lumpur, I spent the day with Healer Man and a few of his friends. Later that night we were alone together, and I knew it was time for me to set some boundaries. As I approached the conversation, I could feel my nerves and lack of confidence, a true indication that I was stepping in to a new way of being.

I told him that I was looking forward to our friendship moving in another direction, a healthier direction, and that what had gone on during the past few months wasn't ok. I was looking forward to our friendship looking differently. I was struggling to stand firm in my power during this talk, and he came back with some comments of why he was so frustrated and so on. The conversation continued, and I realized a complete agreement wasn't going to happen. Although I could have stood more in my power and said more, I am proud that I took the step in harnessing this new way of being - I guess practice makes perfect.

What I really discovered is that when you step out of a pattern and do something, anything, for the first time, you are going to be a bit clumsy and the idea of doing things correctly or saying the right thing the very first time isn't realistic. What I know and what has been true for me is that when I continue to do it (in this case set boundaries of what I will no longer be accepting in my life), it gets easier, your confidence gets strong and you learn the right language.

So setting my boundaries with Healer Man wasn't perfect, but I did it. Although it was scary, it was exactly what I needed to do.

The next morning I boarded a plane to Thailand, where I would spend the next three months. Throughout the previous six months something inside me knew this piece of my journey was going to be big, and I was excited to finally discover what was in store for me.

The Spiritual Journey Exercise
Theme: Healthy Relationships

———————— ❧ ————————

I HAD LEFT Canada and therefore had time away from my familiar life and time away from Healer Man. Meditating, connecting to myself and God, and being around women I love and resonate with brought me back on path.

Although I had done a lot of work and healing on myself, I slipped off path and back into familiar ways. I was no longer on my own priority list. Meditation and connection allowed me to really see how out of alignment I was. Something needed to be done about it. I needed to speak my truth to Healer Man, set boundaries, and begin to practice self-love and care again.

This exercise is your checkpoint, a time to reflect on where you have gone off path or slipped back in to old, familiar ways. It is also a good time to see what is really working and what you need to continue and/or do more of.

Give yourself the time to ask yourself the following questions:

1. What relationships in your life are you particularly proud of and happy with?
2. What relationships in your life do you miss and crave more of?
3. What relationships in your life no longer serve you and need to change?
4. Who deserves more of your time?

5. Who do you need to give less of your time to?
6. Are you aligned with your spiritual principles, values and desired feelings?

Take Action!

So now that you know who you desire to spend more of your time with and who you have to create more distance between it is time to act.

Your homework is:

- Reach out to the person or people whose presence in your life you are happy and grateful for and let them know. Tell them how much you appreciate and are grateful for their relationship.
- Contact the person or people whom you miss and desire a stronger and bigger relationship with. Let them know how much they mean to you and that you desire a deeper connection with them.
- Speak up and set boundaries with the person or people whose relationship and presence in your life no longer contributes to your life in a positive and meaningful way.

This homework is simple but not easy; it requires great courage and vulnerability. Although having these conversations is hard, they are necessary in order to really welcome in and receive the connection and love we all are searching for.

And remember, get back in to alignment with your spiritual principles, values and feelings. They are the things that guide and give light along the unknown path.

Way to go my brave and beautiful soul. Keep going you are doing so well!

CHAPTER 11

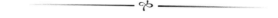

A Feminine & Sexual Opening

AFTER ONE PLANE ride, two taxis, a ferry and a scooter ride (with my 80 pound bag), I arrived, during the rainy season, on the island that would be my home for the next three months.

Just a couple of days after arriving, I began a one-month yoga intensive. It consisted of yoga twice a day, two hours each session, for six days a week. After every afternoon session there was an hour lecture on various yogic topics such as different types of cleansing, solar and lunar energies, vegetarianism, morals and ethics, brahmacharya (sexual continence) and urine therapy.

Throughout the first week, my awareness heightened of how tight and closed down I had become. There has always been a part of me that longed for true connection but yet pushed it away at the same time. Along with this came with my insecurity and self-loathing that focused around my body. There I was, the second or third biggest girl in the class surrounded by tiny yoga bodies.

All my 'shit' was laid out on full display, and I was overwhelmed by wondering if it ever gets easier. Will these walls and insecurities ever stop appearing or holding me back from feeling good and having what I desire?

So I continued with the yoga and shed a few tears while I was in class as I could feel some of the tightness and tension release from my body. I slowly began to spend time with others in my class, trying to be conscious of reaching out and not retreating (literally) to my old ways.

Things didn't feel as if they were 'flowing' as I expected them to be. I had had a strong feeling, a knowing, about Thailand and knew that this place was going to have a lot for me, but in the beginning I wasn't feeling it. Was I wrong? Why wasn't it so easy? By the time the one month intensive was over, it felt great not to be holding so much tension in my body and to be making a few connections. But ultimately, I felt that by the end of my three months I'd be ready to leave.

As my one month intensive ended and my first week-long tantra course began, I started to ask around about yoni massage. Since Healer Man had been to this same school, he was the first to tell me about it. Yoni is Sanskrit for vagina, meaning sacred place. A woman's yoni can hold tension like just like every other area of our body.

Too many women in this world have experienced sexual trauma, and many more have suppressed their sensuality and their sexual selves. Yoni massage is a beautiful tool to help women work through these and other issues. The goal of a yoni massage isn't necessarily to have an orgasm, but rather to let yourself feel and open to what arises in a safe space where you don't have to perform. Often, women can get very emotional during and/or after the massage because of what is coming up for them.

I am fortunate enough to not have any history of sexual abuse, but I would say my sensuality and sexuality have been suppressed.

So I booked my first yoni massage with a well-known and respected female therapist. I arrived not feeling nervous but feeling really ready. The room was adorned with sarongs, lights, candles, pictures of prominent spiritual people and incense was burning. It was a very beautiful, spiritual and hippie type of place which made me feel very comfortable both in the space and with her.

As I sat down, she asked me a few questions. Knowing this was my first experience, she walked me through the entire process.

The first step was that as I undress, I make an intention of what I want to release with each piece of clothing. As I removed my clothes, I made the intention of releasing shyness, shame, and frigidity, until I was there naked before her as I just shared all the negative stuff I carried around with me that I no longer wanted to hold on to.

I then lay down and was given a full body massage. As she massaged me with coconut oil, she even gave my body a couple compliments that I didn't know how to respond to or receive; I just said an awkward "Thank you."

I then turned over on my back and she continued to massage my entire body, avoiding my breasts at first, but then incorporating them into the massage. I felt relaxed, open and near the beginnings of pleasure. She then focused on some pressure points on my stomach before she moved closer to my yoni. The outside of my yoni began to get massaged and specific pressure points were focused on as was well.

Then came the moment when she asked me tighten my yoni muscles (Kegels anyone?), and as I released and breathed out her fingers entered me. Just as there are pressure points outside the yoni, there are pressure points inside as well, and she put pressure on all of them, one o'clock, three o'clock, five o'clock, seven o'clock and eleven o'clock. The pressure should be at an eight on a scale of ten, not too painful but enough to begin to release tension and built up energy.

When that was over, she began to focus on different spots inside my yoni: G-spot, A-spot, and cervix. There are even spots that I had never heard of like the P-spot and kundalini spot. She spent time on each area, but the spot where I felt the most pleasure was the A spot, and as she focused solely on that spot, my energy began to rise and I experienced a full body orgasm. As I began to come down from my climax I could feel the energy move throughout my entire body. My lips were tight and vibrating and my hands clamped together from all the energy.

I laid there for at least ten minutes so the energy could subside and so I could actually walk out of there. As I got up she brought me my clothes, but this time I was to make an intention of what I wanted to bring in and take with me as I put on each piece of clothing. As I got dressed, I made the intention to bring in confidence, sensuality and pleasure, and there I was fully clothed again but in some way different, ignited. I gave my therapist a hug, thanked her, and then went on my way. I felt so good after my yoni massage, not only ignited, but fresh almost as if I had started to return to my natural state.

This feeling of invigoration and connection with my sensuality got me even more excited and ready for my first week of Tantra.

I walked into the yoga hall on the first day of the tantra course wearing my yoga capri pants and a light 3/4 length baseball type t-shirt with very little make-up. Now this is a tantric yoga school where everyone is very loving and affectionate with each other and I longed to be a part of it, yet at the same time my guard was up, deflecting the love and affection that was so abundant.

I was excited to start the workshop until I started to notice myself amongst the other participants, especially the women - they were in dresses, ultra-feminine, and they moved in a way that told me they loved their bodies.

I approached the female teacher and explained to her how I was noticing how rigid I was and how I was putting a guard up to experiencing the very thing I came to experience, connection. I was getting frustrated. I felt so willing to connect with others but when it came to actually doing it I froze and became confused by not knowing how, even though I clearly saw the opportunity in front of me.

When the teacher and I were discussing these insecurities and inadequacies, she acknowledged how important my awareness was of them and how I could now make another choice. By making a conscious choice I could begin to allow in the affection and feel sensual as a woman.

She then gave me homework: masturbation. She said to begin to connect with my body, observe pleasure and begin to embrace my sexual energy. I felt shy as she was talking, which I observed and knew I had to push through to get to a place where I could really own and feel proud of myself, my body and my sensuality.

Devoting well over an hour to self-pleasure and masturbation was such a foreign idea, but I was here to break out of my old patterns, so "masturbation here I come!"

I carved out time for my homework in the middle of the day during the workshop break. I played sensual music and had a hot shower. I stepped out of the shower and back into my room where candles were lit, took off my bathrobe, and lay down on my bed with a bottle of coconut oil on the end table. I lay there focusing on my breath as I began to slowly touch and trace various parts of my body, my legs, hips, stomach and breasts. I had to remind myself to come back to the present moment and keep focusing on my breath because I had many thoughts.

I opened the jar of coconut oil, filled my hands and begun to spread it over my body. It felt good to show my own body this amount of love and affection. I began to give it love, and the way I viewed my body changed. I looked down at my body and loved the smoothness and the curves that I saw. As I continued to caress and really feel my body, I noticed my increased enjoyment and as I touched my breasts and yoni my pleasure began to build.

Although I did not climax, the time that I took infused my body with self-love, care and pleasure. I felt calm, sensual and juicy afterwards, and

I could see these feelings when I looked at myself in the mirror. I returned to class ready to dive in.

This first tantra course had many lectures that were filled with tons of wisdom and information as well as exercises that had us all pair up.

One lecture that I particularly loved was about Shakti (divine feminine) and Shiva (divine masculine). It described how Shiva provides stability and direction while the feminine, Shakti, creates and manifests. We learned that men (Shiva) and women (Shakti) have different attributes but both are of equal value. I loved that.

One exercise in particular had Shiva, the male partner, sit up straight with his legs straight out and slightly open while the woman sat the same way on top of her Shiva. When both partners were sitting up straight, face to face with their torsos close to one another, we placed our hands on our partner's root chakra (or as close as possible) and began to breathe deeply and quickly. While this was happening, music that resonated on that chakra played in the background, and after a certain amount of time we moved our hands upward to the next chakra long with the music. By the time we reached the top chakras, I'd been breathing quite heavily with my partner while being physically very close. Just through the breath it could be very easy to have an orgasm, never mind the intimacy of holding a partner so close - in fact the couple next to me both were able to have an orgasm, and the whole room knew about it, which probably prevented a few people (myself included) from achieving their own orgasms.

After being in a room of 30 couples doing this exercise, I would say I got a lot more comfortable with affection and sexuality.

As the week came to an end, I noticed how I began to allow myself to enjoy the affection from others, to get dressed up even if it was just for class, and to feel sexy. Progress is progress.

As you can imagine, this school and community holds a lot of sexual energy, and there is a lot of opportunity to 'practice' both sexual and non-sexual aspects of tantra. Mr. Lover Lover and I were out one evening along with group from the workshop. We began talking, and he invited me to spend the day with him on the other side of the island.

We went out to a popular beach together, and he was very affectionate with me. Even though I had moved through some modesty during tantra, I was initially very uncomfortable with the amount of affection he gave me. I was cautious of what others would think and worried it could make people feel uncomfortable. He would just stop while we were walking and kiss me. I was flattered but not totally present because my shyness flared up. He was also very complimentary towards me, which I had a difficult time accepting.

The first time we were together, he started by giving me an entire full body massage; this was very different from the Western men I had been with before. He was so gentle and soft with me and would take the time to kiss me, all over; my pleasure came first. We made love for hours, and it was beautiful. I felt so respected by him.

Throughout our limited time together, I began to open up and embrace the affection. I noticed that I was less concerned with what others thought. Slowly I managed to take in and be grateful for the compliments he would give me.

Our last night together was a beautiful ending to our brief encounter. Experiencing so much affection and having a man look at my naked body and tell me that I was a true Shakti with a beautiful body was heart-opening and transformative. It was a powerful meeting, and the shortness of our interaction had nothing to do with how divine and heart opening it was for me and I hope for him as well.

Throughout my time in Thailand, my father and I had been exchanging emails, finalizing and confirming details of the week I would spend with him and his family. His two teenage daughters had no idea they had a nearly 30-year-old sister, and I was concerned how they would react. Not to mention that they would then learn that I would be arriving soon to spend a week with them.

At Christmas my dad told his parents and sister that we had reconnected, and they were a bit surprised but supportive.

Soon after, I got an email saying that earlier that day my dad and step mom had sat their two girls down and told them that they had a sister and that she was coming in just a few weeks to meet and spend a week with them.

I was out. I was no longer hidden, a secret, or something to be ashamed of. The little girl within me had been waiting years for that invite and email from her dad.

Things were shifting; old patterns and stories were dropping away in front of me. I was thrilled to see these old ways and beliefs dropped away and curious what the dropping away would reveal.

An all-women's workshop was next on my list, and even though I was just beginning to open up, I had huge resistance to participating. I know that I need to work on my blockage to developing friendships with other women, and this workshop confirmed my own knowing.

As I walked into the space on the first day, I could feel my chest and whole body tighten. I was scared, and for me the fear was more evident than the love.

There can be such an underlying sense of competition and judgement between women, and we can be really good at being cruel towards one another. I could remember so many times where I felt drawn to certain women but couldn't express my appreciation to them for fear I was perhaps "below them." There were also times where I did judge other women when they were reflecting to me something I didn't like or was ignoring in myself. I wanted to reach out and connect, but in many ways I felt paralyzed and unsure of what taking this initial step looked like.

A beautiful woman in the workshop mentioned how she wanted to open up to receiving in her life, and this completely resonated with me. Feminine energy is receptive, which is why we are so emotional and sensitive. I realized that by pushing away and not seeing the value in feminine energy, I couldn't receive what I desired to manifest in my life. From that point on, I made a choice to let in and embrace the divine feminine.

I sat down and had a power meditation where I let go and made an intention to embrace my true feminine. During that time, the message I received was, "Welcome home."

My perception shifted as I began to look at all the women in the course with such love and appreciation and saw the gifts we all had to offer.

It was time to let in and connect with other women and with my own femininity, which I had been ignoring for so long. I felt like I was finally starting to get some things right.

I had a lot going on; a lot was changing, and I felt as though I was getting the momentum and courage to really open up and move through a lot of fear.

I had heard about many things in the tantric community I was living in, one being a list of 'active' men and women who are open to having a relationship or a lover to practice sexual tantra. I had learned from class about how healing sex can be, and, in particular, how women, if we're in the right space and with the right partner, can begin to heal and open up sexually. I was ready to open up.

I approached my tantra teacher and asked if there was anyone in the community who could assist me in opening sexually, and she mentioned a couple men who are quite senior in the community. So I made an appointment to meet with one of them.

When I arrived, we first took some time to talk about me and why I had come. I asked a few questions around moving through family/ancestral patterns and then asked about moving through insecurities. I mentioned how helpful taking the tantra workshops had been, but that I was still feeling constricted and completely insecure about my body. He mentioned that many men would love my voluptuous figure and that many would love to transfigure with my body. Transfiguration is a tantric term that means to see the divine, true essence of the person in front of you and witness their inner Shakti or Shiva as you gaze at them.

He then offered to transfigure my naked body.

I responded, surprised, "Is that something we could do?"

"Yes," he said, and we both smiled. Although I agreed to undress in front of this man for transfiguration, I knew that at some point we'd probably be sleeping together. He then gave me his phone number so we could make a time to get together.

I was surprised and thrilled with myself. Who was this woman? It was as if something was immersing within me; a sexy and fearless woman who just goes after what she wants. I could get used to this.

As I was on a roll with being brave and trying new things, I learned that my yoni massage therapist was holding a women-only workshop.

The workshop was set up in a way where you and your partner would give each other a yoni massage. I was terrified, so I decided to do it.

Knowing I needed to open up more, especially with other women, I thought this would be my opportunity. This, of course was met with huge resistance and fear, and I even tried to get out of it by finding my partner someone else to go with. However, in the end, I showed up.

There were twelve women, six couples, all in the same room. I offered, (quite selfishly I'll admit) to go first, thinking I would be naked in front of everyone for the least amount of time possible. However, the Universe is clever, and it didn't really turn out that way. We were all asked to stand in a circle and we would each, one by one, make an intention of what we wanted to release with each piece of clothing we removed. Then we'd go around the circle as long as we needed to until we were all naked. The women giving the yoni massage first were to keep their underwear on.

So each woman, one by one, went around and shared one thing she wanted to release as she removed a piece of clothing. When I heard women express the shame and insecurities they were so desperate to release, I felt less alone. I also felt such sadness, as I heard the sexual trauma that some of the women were hoping to get rid of.

There came the moment where it was my turn to remove my shirt and reveal the large burn-like birthmark that covers my entire left arm. I could feel the hesitation in my chest — this was the moment I was dreading. As I removed my shirt and placed it on the floor beside me, I could see that all the other women noticed it and then met me with smiles and loving gazes. A healing occurred.

As we all stood there naked and looking at each other, I saw women of different shapes and sizes and found them all beautiful. Naked women are beautiful. We all looked around at each other with such love. To be where women are so loving and supportive of one another manifested such power that I could almost touch it, and I believe it did something for women everywhere.

I was initially nervous about giving my partner a yoni massage. I didn't know if I could hold the space for her while she was in such a vulnerable position. As the massage continued and the facilitator kept giving directions and guidance, I looked at my partner, the woman in front of me, and felt such love and protection towards her. It was such a privilege to witness such a healing and to have another woman trust me in that way.

I thought to myself, "This is something I could do."

It was then my turn and by this time, I felt so safe and cared for by the other women in the room that I went into it fully open and ready to receive whatever was to come my way.

Once we were all done, we stayed unclothed in a circle, shared our experiences and hugged one another. It was beautiful and powerful. Experiences like these that hold such much magic and divinity cannot be explained, but I know and I could feel that something had shifted for every woman in the room.

Immediately after the yoni massage workshop, I left to go see the senior tantric teacher for my sexual opening. I was nervous, my heart was pounding, and I was also late, so I was rushing to see him yet resistant at the same time. I approached the door with my body still covered in coconut oil from the massage, I heard a 'come in' and I opened the door and stood in the entrance way.

He walked in the room, immediately approached me, and without wasting one moment he kissed me passionately and we headed towards the bedroom. I was still nervous and although this was happening a lot more quickly than I anticipated, I went with it. I was naked within seconds.

He immediately went down on me and then began to kiss me again, stopping only to say affirmations like "You are so much of a woman" and "beautiful Shakti."

While we made love, he checked with me to see how I was feeling. I felt tight and constricted inside, which was slightly painful. He was careful, slowing down when I needed him to and continually checking in with how and what I was feeling.

At points we would slow down, and then I would feel an increase in energy and continue. During moments like these he would get me to affirm out loud "It's building."

There was a moment where we were moving around, changing positions, and I was holding myself up and he asked me to surrender and fall back. As I did that his hand and arm were behind me, while he moved me, it was a small but beautiful moment of Shakti surrendering to Shiva.

Once we were finished making love, we lay there together, and he gently grabbed my head and said, "You have no idea what this [lovemaking] will do for up here."

I didn't really think anything of it. He then mentioned how a lot of energy moved and that I may be sore for the next few days and once that is done, he and I should meet again. I agreed.

I then got dressed and was given a kiss goodbye. I went home, tired from my eventful day of a group yoni massage and a sexual opening. I fell asleep immediately.

I woke up in the middle of the night, which never happens to me, with my head covered in sweat, my hair drenched. I wondered "What is going on?" and since I didn't know what to do I went back to sleep.

The next day I pondered what had happened. My thought was that something was ignited, awakened and all that energy was rushing to my head and therefore, my crown chakra. I continued my normal routine of attending yoga class, but as I sat in class like I had done for months, I noticed that something was different. Men in my class kept looking at me, some even smiling; my instant thought was "What did this guy do? He is good!"

I met with this man a few more times, and if my time in Thailand had not been ending, I would have continued until I reached my full potential as an orgasmic woman. I enjoyed the beginning of my opening, feeling the real me beginning to emerge and having a man see this part of me break open, the real me.

I began the next level of the tantra workshops, which for the first time ever had more men than women - thank you God! There were many activities and exercises that we did that left no room for comfort.

One of the first exercises related to our bodies: how we feel about them and what we are most insecure about. The exercise had us form a group of four, and because God is funny, I was the only female in my group. We took turns telling our fellow group members what area of our bodies we felt most insecure about. We then lay down as the others massaged and sent love to that one particular area.

When it was my turn, I told the three men that I was most self-conscious and insecure about my stomach (muffin top anyone?). I then lay down as all three men began to massage my stomach. Initially I had to take a few big, conscious breaths as the thing I loathed most about my body was getting the most attention. As the massaging continued, I started to really feel the love that was being sent my way. My stomach was hungry for this affection as though it had never received this level of love before, which was probably true.

As the exercise came to an end, we all shared our experience and feedback for one another. One man thought we were all crazy, including me, about our insecurities and turned to me and said I was "luscious" and that he wanted to bite into me like a juicy burger! This made me smile, and I felt a bit more lighthearted about my body and insecurities.

Another exercise had us partner up and touch ourselves while our partner followed our hand. Then we took our partner's hand and placed it on our body where we wanted to be touched, culminating with the final stage where we expressed verbally to our partner where we wanted them to touch us. Voicing my desire about what I wanted and having it be all about me in that moment was incredibly uncomfortable, but I chose to power through. You know you have moved through inhibitions and frigidity when you are straddling a man and circling and grinding your hips against his in a group of 100 people and when it's your turn you ask him to pin up your hands, pull your hair and bite you — if that isn't progress I don't know what is!

One of the exercises that really stirred up some insecurity was where we were asked to write out our deepest fantasy. I naively wrote out mine thinking that we would just be keeping them for ourselves, but no no no... we were then asked to form a group and throw our paper into the centre of the circle. A member of the group randomly grabbed a piece of paper and read out the fantasy while the whole group guessed who wrote it. My heart sank. So we all went around hearing the fantasies of others and guessing who's belonged to whom. Then came my turn. I have no poker face, especially in situations like this. As one of the group members started to read out a fantasy of a woman sleeping with her older boss, then having wild passionate sex in public places and him worshiping her while she made love to him, I was cringing and my face was red. It was an easy guess for my group to say the least. That exercise took me a day or two to get over; I felt exposed, yet I knew there was no judgement from anyone else and that it was just me criticizing myself. As time went on and I reflected, I found it really freeing to have had that side of myself expressed because I had never told anyone, including my intimate partners.

Although I was being challenged to move through some serious inhibitions and insecurities, I liked what was starting to occur with me. I felt wild and free, and I loved it. I felt safe in that environment and loved how we were all comfortable with each other and could share and express such intimate things knowing there was no judgement, only love and acceptance.

During the final ceremony of the tantra course, we conducted a ritual and there was a moment where the men stayed seated while the women stood up and took a particular pose. We were to stand there and be adored and worshiped by our male partner.

By this time in the course and in the ritual I felt so feminine, juicy and full of love. My heart was opening, and I could feel that I was in total alignment with God, exactly where I needed to be and that I had finally arrived to the place I had been searching for.

During this moment in the ritual I felt so alive. I was completely present throughout this ritual and there was a moment towards the end where we all sat in a circle and were guided through a beautiful meditation where both the Shaktis and Shivas were honored. I sat there and observed myself and how I was feeling. I felt complete contentment and happiness. In that moment, I just felt good in all aspects. I felt completely aligned to my true and authentic self, so much so that I allowed the tears of relief and joy to flow. It was a moment where nothing else mattered; all my worries were gone and even when I thought about them they weren't worries at all. I expressed my gratitude for everyone and everything that had brought me to this moment. This is how I want to want to feel and this is who I want to be, this beautiful woman. I felt so adored and cherished by God.

The last (and first) time I had felt this sense of bliss, I was 19 and I was with my brother Nicholas at his school play. I by no means had a lot of money or any direction in my life but I was so happy. When I think back to that moment and the moment in the ritual there is one common thread — my brother Nicholas, the brave and divine catalyst who brought me to this moment and continues to guide me.

During this state of bliss and gratitude I often found myself turning to God, saying, "You thought I was worthy of all this? Thank you thank you thank you".

Tantra ignited my opening, and I felt a desire to experience even more, but in a more intimate, physical and active way.

There was one tantric man whom I found very attractive. I had an interest in"practicing" tantra with him. I was nervous and my fear of rejection surfaced, but when I found out that he was "active," I was encouraged by my tantra teacher to approach him.

One evening we both were at the same event, and when I saw him alone, I thought to myself "This is your time to do it." I nervously approached him and mentioned that I had spoken to one of the tantra teachers and that I knew he was 'active' and I was wondering if he would initiate me into tantra. My heart sank because I had just stepped through a huge fear, but then he responded with a smile and a 'yes,' and we made a plan to get into contact and make a time to meet.

I left that conversation thinking to myself "Oh my god, I can't believe I just blatantly asked someone to sleep with me!"

I then gave myself credit for having had the guts to do it and acknowledged my inner changes and shifts that must have occurred for me to approach him.

A day or two later he contacted me to meet up, and we arranged for me to come to his place. I arrived, legs shaved, makeup and matching underwear on and Brazilian wax done! We first sat down, and he asked me what I was hoping to get out of and/or experience from our encounter. I told him how I am moving through some inhibitions and that I thought an experience like this could help me move through those barriers and open up even more.

We then went in to his room and placed flowers and chocolates on his alter as an offering. We sat down crossed legged in front of each other and made a consecration, offering the fruits of this meeting to the divine, and then we did a short transfiguration (gazing at the divine within one another) together, which created a beautiful and safe space.

He then asked me to stand up and undress in front of him, and my heart sank. I began by removing my skirt, placing it to the side. Next it was time to remove my shirt, which is always a vulnerable moment for me because of the birthmark.

As I began to remove my shirt, I told him that he would notice my birthmark, that it looks like a burn but it doesn't hurt, but he paid no attention to what I was saying and my obvious insecurity. I breathed deeply and removed my shirt and put it to the side; I was then standing in only my underwear, which was next to be taken off. I removed my bra and then slid off my underwear; there I was completely naked and feeling totally vulnerable in front of a man that I hardly knew and found very attractive. He then looked over and transfigured my entire naked body. As I looked at him while he looked over me, I saw a wonderment and appreciation in his eyes as he, Shiva adored and appreciated the Shakti (me) standing in front of him. Then he asked me to turn around, "No way" is what I said to myself but then I took another huge breath and turned around, and as he scanned and transfigured the rest of my body, my heart was racing.

Once he was done, I turned around as he stood up, approached me, and kissed me. We had a beautiful evening of lovemaking.

I felt fully present during our evening together and was grateful for such a powerful and beautiful experience. Once the evening was done we said goodbye, and I left a different woman than the one I was when I arrived.

I had been fully seen with all my beauty and flaws, which took away my insecurities and left me feeling empowered.

I felt so alive, so confident, so wild, like who I really was had finally begun to emerge. I was on a roll and wanted to keep the momentum going.

There was another, well-experienced tantra teacher whom I decided to approach. I had a bit of a crush on him, to be quite honest. He and I had spoken previously, and he had given me some great advice around stepping even more strongly in to my femininity.

He was in an open relationship and had at least two partners I knew of and with him being tantric I thought why not ask him. I sent him a text message mentioning how he and I had talked about my opening up more, both physically and sexually. I asked him if he was willing to help me out with this and hit send. I was terrified.

The next day I got my reply; he said yes and made a time for us to meet.

He requested that I come with no make-up and no perfume, just me, completely bare, so that's how I arrived at his house.

He asked me what my expectations were from our time together, and I found myself not knowing what to say. I went over what we had previously discussed and how I felt ready to open up and ignite my sexuality. We continued to talk, and he mentioned that he would love to make love to me but that he had to remain celibate for the next week because of a program or ritual he was participating in.

He mentioned he would give me a yoni massage but invited me to 'play' with him. We started by making a consecration, offering all the fruits of our meeting to the divine. I then made myself comfortable on the bed and we began to kiss.

He then undressed me, leaving only my underwear on, and started to massage my full body as I lay down on my back on the bed. He asked me to let him know when he was doing something that I enjoyed; expressing what I liked was something I found really difficult to do. As he continued to massage me he gently grabbed and massaged my stomach, "I like when you do that," I said with my voice slightly quivering.

Before long, I was fully naked, and we continued fooling around and being playful. He complimented every, and I mean every, part of my body. Both myself and my body were so revered; I felt truly worshipped. Being held in such high regard and feeling so much pleasure was a heavenly experience.

It was quite intense for both of us, and although he kept to his commitment to be celibate, he did share that it was hard to keep his underwear on. I wanted him so badly.

His entered me with his finger, and I was warmed up, to say the least, my back beginning to arch in pleasure. As he continued showing me his expertise in this area, he asked "Have you ever had a squirting orgasm?"

I replied, "No."

"Well, you will today." He then grabbed my legs and pulled me down so that my bum was at the edge of the bed. His fingers inside me, his rhythm increased, and I was about to peak. I then looked down towards my yoni, shocked to find I was experiencing female ejaculation. Witnessing it distracted me from the orgasm I was experiencing, but I couldn't look away; I was in awe.

As I came down from my orgasm, he made sure I was holding on to all of this sexual energy by imploding my orgasm, and he then helped move the energy up to my higher chakras, saying, "Give it back up to God."

When I came back and got myself grounded and dressed, I asked him "What was that?" as I pointed to the mess left on the floor. He mentioned that the more I make love and pleasure myself, the quicker it will happen. I was still in disbelief that I was able to ejaculate.

I thanked him, we gave each other a kiss and a loving hug, and then I was on my way.

I arrived home feeling juicy, sensual and alive. I wanted to hold on to this feeling forever. It felt as though I, my true self was awakening and all my masks, stories and limitations were dropping away.

I was in my last days on this island, but I didn't want to leave. The orgasmic woman who had been hidden away was beginning to be unleashed.

However, my time in Thailand and in this community was up and it was time to go. My blossoming had just begun, but now it was time to move on to my next stop, a week in China with my dad.

Nothing I can do or say can express the amount of blessings and gratitude I have felt for this island, this community and every soul who has touched my heart. I am different from when I arrived. I have woken up. Woken up to the truth of who I am and what resides within me.

I knew I had changed when I left my bungalow wearing a belly shirt. I was a bit nervous at first, but still, I went out showing off the curves and softness of my stomach.

I had been called by the Universe to break away from the path I had been on. To understand, now, that this is what was planned for me makes me want to weep with gratitude. Knowing that this experience was lined up just for me makes me feel a level of love that humbles me and brings me to my knees.

It was worth it. All of it.

Feminine & Sexual Opening Exercise
Theme: Femininity & Sexuality

————— ✿ —————

TANTRA RESONATED WITH me on so many levels; it made me feel connected, alive and as though I had retuned home. It was as though everything that I had experienced had brought me to this place for the experiences I needed most.

Embracing and operating from my femininity, exploring my sensuality, and connecting with other women brought me back to a bigger truth, showing me my power, divinity, purpose and limitless love and capacity.

The following exercises will challenge you to experience your femininity, explore your sensuality and connect to other women.

1. How do you define femininity? What does it look like? What value does femininity have?
2. View yourself fully and completely in your feminine.
   - What do you look like?
   - What are you wearing?
   - How do you feel?
   - How does it taste?
   - How do you smell?
   - How do you move?
   - What energy are you radiating?

3. What makes you feel sexy? What daily things can you be doing to increase your sensuality and feeling of sexiness? For example, you could wear sexy underwear underneath your work clothes/ uniform.
4. List your most treasured female connections. How can you depend on these connections? If you do not have any, ask yourself which women in your life do you desire a deeper connection with? In what ways can you reach out and create an opportunity to connect?

Take Action!
This homework is extra important because it begins to ignite your sexual energy, so give yourself the time you deserve.

-   Act from and be in your feminine energy. Align yourself to the feminine woman you described above. Start to wear more feminine clothing, wear sexy underwear, pay attention to how you move, and start dancing! Yes, that's right, I want you to dance everyday for one week. Observe how your body moves and give yourself permission to move and let go. Also, look at what you wrote in question two above and begin to incorporate some of those qualities in to your daily life.
-   Connect with women. Make a time to connect with a girlfriend or girlfriends, girls only! *Vulnerability alert* During this time share with them something that you've always wanted to say or share but never could. If your struggle is to connect and develop female friendships then let them know that and ask if you can meet up again and more often. Also, express and share your gratitude and let them know what kind of impact it had on you.
-   Experience pleasure. Everyday for one week you are tasked with performing self pleasure. Through masturbation we begin to get our sexual energy flowing; we begin to infuse our body with love and

start on our way to becoming an orgasmic women. When we begin to feel pleasure our standards begin to raise and we can't go back.

Once we become orgasmic in one area of our life we become orgasmic in all areas of our life.

Once we become an orgasmic woman our life becomes orgasmic.

Congratulations, you are now well on your way to living an orgasmic life!

CHAPTER 12

—— ✛ ——

Ending the Story

I SAID GOOD bye to my beautiful island home. I was very sad to go and desperately wanted to stay, but I knew how important my next adventure was. After 29 years of longing to know and have a relationship with my dad, I had finally received my invitation.

I made a little stop in Bali for a couple of days before I headed off to see my dad, stepmom and two new little sisters. I spent some time with friends and shared all my juicy and vulnerable stories. I felt alive and happy like I never had before. Reminiscing about some of my experiences, especially those that took true courage, filled me with love and a sense of pride. Although there were moments of risk and vulnerability, those were the stories that inspired the most joy. My entire body felt joyful and orgasmic.

I met with my therapist and shared my experiences with her, and we discussed the next leg of my journey. I felt really ready to spend this week with my dad and his family. It seemed as though I might be fully and truly embraced.

A grown woman rather than a wounded little girl was arriving for this week. Although my inner child was with me and excited, my adult self was in the driver's seat. I felt as though my expectations were realistic. As an almost 30-year-old woman, the relationship I was now going to be developing with my dad was going to look and feel different than if I had grown up with him. I thought the relationship would develop more as a friendship rather than a traditional father-daughter relationship, and I felt at peace with that.

My therapist mentioned that this visit would change me. I had never thought of it that way, but how could it not? So much of my energy and beliefs were tied to the stories I told myself about my father.

I said goodbye to my friends and stepped towards the week I had been waiting a very long time for.

I arrived at the Macau, China, airport where my dad and the older of his two girls picked me up. I was greeted with a big hug, first from my dad and then from one of my new sisters. It was a big moment for all of us, but no one really knew what to say or how to navigate through the enormity of the circumstance. When we arrived at their

apartment, I was given a big hug from my step mom and met my very shy and reserved sister who also greeted me with a hug. There was a lot of nervous energy but I felt very welcomed.

As we all moved through the first few days, the shyness, formality and awkwardness remained. Still, I felt very cared for and considered as they took me around and showed me the sights.

My inner child came out to play as one day my sisters were hitting a balloon back and forth to each other and asked me to join in. I was happy to be included in playing with them. It was a beautiful bonding experience that allowed for our silliness to shine through.

As the week progressed, things became a lot more relaxed and comfortable, and we were all able to be ourselves. The normality of my sisters arguing in front of me at the dinner table was so refreshing.

There were some real learnings and realizations for me during the week. My dad has all girls and no boys. I wondered if he ever secretly wanted boys.

Throughout my upbringing, it was my experience that boys were preferred. Having been raised with two younger brothers, I could see the preference and pride their father had in only conceiving boys. When girls were born in my family, it felt like there was an energy of disappointment amongst the men.

There was one moment during the week when my stepmom shared a story of their travels throughout Asia about how a woman had approached them and asked, "Oh you have two girls, you try again for a boy?"

One of my sisters said, "Why would she say that?"

I thought to myself, "Wow she never grew up feeling less-than because she is a girl."

Seeing that my sisters didn't have those feelings of self-doubt was emotional for me. I was out for dinner and had to hold back the tears at this realization because I felt that I had really missed out on that feeling of equality. I asked myself who I would have been if I had been raised with a sense of equal importance to men.

Another realization that hit me was that as it appeared to me, there was and is no emphasis on my sisters' looks, especially body image. When I was growing up I always felt pressure to look a certain way and be a certain weight. When I did gain weight, it was pointed out to me and suggested that I lose a few pounds. My body image continues to be something I struggle with today.

Being female and feeling "less than" because of it along with body image have been my two main struggles. Why did I have to miss out on these experiences? I pondered that question for a while. However, I realized that even if my father had been there during my upbringing, he would have been in his late teens and early 20s, very different than the father he was to my two sisters.

Loving my body and embracing the values and gifts of being female is something I continue to learn and relearn. I guess I missed out on these experiences for a reason. The lack of these experiences has led me to search for greater worth and self-love. Perhaps without it I wouldn't have found my bliss in Thailand.

I remember my therapist offering the advice that I should observe my dad and see what qualities and traits I received from him. Even though he wasn't around when I was growing up, I would have inherited certain genetic qualities from him.

So, I observed him throughout the week and tried to pick out these shared qualities. I noticed my dad was solid and dependable, a true leader. I saw that he gave order and guidance and that it came from a place of love. I remember looking back on the many times I played this role within my family, especially when my brother died. I'd always wonder where that grounded and solid place within me came from and now I knew.

My dad places an importance on leadership, and I have always found this subject interesting and hugely important. Observing this, I was so grateful that I share these qualities with him.

I noticed some physical things as well. Many of my facial features, like my nose and lips, I got from my dad. My body shape is another; I definitely have some curves and know that didn't come from my mother's side. So I have him and his genetics to thank for being the voluptuous woman that I am.

Observing these qualities in him made them even more evident in me, and it was fascinating to see the puzzle pieces come together.

As I was heading towards my 30th birthday and the end of the first act of my life, I saw so many things coming to an end.

I had identified so strongly with the story of my father not being around and now here he was.

As this full circle week came to an end, I saw this story drop away.

With one story ending and with new tantric experiences revealing a part of myself that I was eager to explore, I wondered who I was in the process of becoming. I wondered who and what would awaken within me and what impact she would have on me and on the world.

Ending The Story Exercise
Theme: End The Story

━━━━━━━━━━━ ೕ ━━━━━━━━━━━

THE WEEK WITH my father made me realize that I could no longer - nor did I want to - continue telling myself and living the story of being unwanted and carrying around all the insecurities and behaviours that stemmed from that belief. It was time to end the story, and all the other stories that I told to and about myself and instead really allow myself to expand into the vastness and greatness that were always there.

This exercise is intended to bring the stories we tell ourselves into our awareness so that we can begin to choose another, more empowering story.

Begin to ask for the unconscious stories you tell yourself to come up and get curious about some limiting stories you tell yourself. Complete the following sentences.

1. One story I believe about myself is...
2. One story that holds me back...
3. The stories I tell myself about myself...

Now is the time to intend to ourselves and God that we no longer allow these stories to have power and influence over us.

1. One story I no longer choose to believe...
2. In order to move out of this stuck place, I will create a new story that tells me...

Take Action!

Now that you are aware of the stories you tell yourself be willing to let them go and commit to having stories that serve you and allow your desires to manifest. Now is the time to rewrite the story, literally.

Select a story you have been telling yourself up until now and re-write the ending. Look at the part of the story that is holding you back or keeping you stuck, the part that says you can't or that you are not smart, good or deserving enough and re- write the ending.

Next, write your story about who you are becoming, the one that is pulling you forward, who is choosing to answer the call upon her life. Incorporate new beliefs and perspectives that are anchored in your spiritual principles, values, and desired feelings.

CHAPTER 13

A New Chapter

THIS JOURNEY HAS not been easy, but answering the call upon my life was worth it. Being called at all has been an honour. To feel and know that I universally matter and that my life is important enough to say no to the status quo is something I must remember and carry with me as I step into the next act of my life.

The last two years of my 20s have demanded from me the acceptance and release of my past. They've asked me to stop holding on to the old and outdated patterns, stories, and limitations.

Although my past is true, the abandonment of the old programming is key to in order to fully embody and experience a higher vibrational life.

Forgiveness is my priority as I enter in to the second act of my life. Forgiving people, choices, circumstance and mostly forgiving myself for all I have done and not done.

For me to truly live a full life, to attract and experience all that I desire, I have to say thank you and goodbye to my history. Entering in this new chapter requires me to show up with nothing in order to receive all that I desire and am worthy of and all that God has planned.

My past and old patterns will no doubt show up again, but it will be my practice of continual surrender, forgiveness, and trust that will take me towards the gifts and abundance of my new chapter.

As I release my attachments to my history, I must remember to show up fully to this next chapter free from my past, free from expectations, and with my heart wide open.

A New Chapter Exercise
Theme: An Open Heart

———— ✿ ————

As THE FIRST act of my life was coming to a close, I began to see how necessary it was to forgive everything and move forward with my heart wide open. This allowed me to envision the possibilities of who I was becoming and the life I was creating.

You've done a lot of work up until this point, so give yourself some credit. In order to heal and step in to the life you desire you have to do your work, so great job!

For our final exercise, visualize yourself already as the woman you desire to be. Ask yourself the following questions and write out the answers:

1. What does she look like?
2. What is she wearing?
3. What does she smell like?
4. What is she feeling?
5. How does she move?
6. What type of energy does she give off?
7. How does she view and feel about herself?
8. How does she view and feel about the world?
9. How does she impact the world?
10. What is her career?

11. What type of relationships is she engaged in?
12. What type of friendships does she have?
13. What type of people does she surround her self with?
14. What kind of food does she eat?
15. What is her spiritual practice?

Now that you have a strong sense of the woman you are stepping into, visualize her right in front of you. Take a moment to look at her and all who she is. After you feel you have spent enough time with her, visualize her turning away from you so that you only see the back of her. Now, with her back towards you step forward and into her, absorbing and becoming all that you have observed of her, knowing that this is now you.

Take a few additional minutes to meditate and allow the energy of this new you to be integrated into your being.

Take Action!

Create a daily spiritual practice for yourself. What will you do for you, every day, that keeps you aligned with your higher power and the woman you now intend to be?

This could include yoga, meditation, prayer, some form of exercise or creative outlet. Know that self care and love is key. So, what will you commit to that connects and serves you and only you?

Once you have your spiritual practice take action! Enjoy your spiritual practice and be proud of the fact that you are now (and always have been) the heroine of your own journey.

Acknowledgements & Gratitude

~ain with you, the reader. With my entire heart, thank you, thank
1 to   ipport and for reading this book and making the coura-
              o a new more fulfilling direction. Knowing that there are
              enough to question the status quo and venture out unto
em-   ills and expands my heart with hope and love.
rld

our   many people who have been with me throughout my jour-
              out them and their support I am unsure where I would be.

ver   om: Thank you for being the agent of change. Without your
ve   teps into the unknown I wouldn't have had the wisdom and
to   eded to be living the joyous life I am living now. I love you
ou
ve

              Tharp, there are no words to capture the impact you and your
              ve had on my life. You have shown me another way and your
              as been unwavering. I love you and thank you.

              dear friends Taren, Melissa, and Aimee: You all have brought
              ove and connection in to my life. Thank you for your continued
              nd unconditional love, may I be blessed enough to be part of
              for lifetimes to come.

              ry, Shannon, Sandy and Kenny: Never have I met such accepting
              erous people, I adore and love you all.

              my brother John, thank you for loving and supporting me even
              earing my sex stories makes you uncomfortable. I love you and will
              be here for you.

To my entire family: Thank you for your love and the lessons that shaped the woman I am today.

Agama Yoga: Thank you for creating the space for my evolutio[n] take flight.

Dear God, thank you for giving me this task, the thought of you de[em]ing me worthy enough to live this life and make an impact on the w[orld] brings me to my knees. May I forever be of service to you and all y[our] children.

And to you Nicholas, you have been the great love of my life. Ne[ver] have I loved someone so much. Thank you for guiding my heart to l[ove] even more. I miss you everyday. May I live in your honour and continu[e to] live a life that is joyous, impactful, filled with meaning and that makes [you] proud. I love you unconditionally, with my whole heart as I always h[ave] and will continue to, for lifetimes.

Made in the USA
San Bernardino, CA
18 December 2017